So You Have to Have a Portfolio

Robert L. Wyatt III • Sandra Looper

So You Have to Have a Portfolio

A Teacher's Guide to Preparation and Presentation

CORWIN PRESS, INC.
A Sage Publications Company
Thousand Oaks, California

For information:

Corwin Press, Inc.
A Sage Publications Company
2455 Teller Road
Thousand Oaks, California 91320
E-mail: order@corwinpress.com

SAGE Publications Ltd.
6 Bonhill Street
London EC2A 4PU
United Kingdom

SAGE Publications India Pvt. Ltd.
M-32 Market
Greater Kailash I
New Delhi 110 048 India

Printed in the United States of America

Library of Congress Cataloging-in-Publication Data

Wyatt, Robert Lee, 1940–
    So you have to have a portfolio: A teacher's guide to
preparation and presentation / Robert L. Wyatt III, Sandra Looper.
        p.   cm.
    Includes bibliographical references and index.
    ISBN 0-8039-6821-3 (cloth: alk. paper)
    ISBN 0-8039-6822-1 (pbk.: alk. paper)
    1. Portfolios in education—United States. 2. Employment
portfolios—United States. 3. Teachers college students—Rating
of—United States.   I. Looper, Sandra.   II. Title.
    LB1728.W93 1999
    370'.71'1—dc21   99-6353

This book is printed on acid-free paper.

    02   03   04   05   10   9   8   7   6   5   4   3

Production Editor: S. Marlene Head
Editorial Assistant: Julia E. Parnell
Typesetter: Rebecca Evans
Cover Designer: Michelle Lee

Contents

Preface

Why We Wrote This Book

Portfolios for assessment in schools of education, and, in fact, in all disciplines in higher education, have become commonplace. The requirements for this somewhat academic assessment are growing with each passing semester. Many states are now requiring teacher education graduates to develop a teaching portfolio. Oklahoma teacher education graduates, for instance, must address 15 competencies mandated by the state legislature and enforced by a commission on higher education. The portfolio shows the commission that educators are prepared to meet the demands of the classroom by reaching the mandated specifications for competency. There are few existing guidelines to assist faculty in the development and assessment of portfolios. Although we found several books on assessment within disciplinary domains, few of those texts crossed over the line to be useful in other areas of learning. Some were directed at professionals wishing to secure promotions, some addressed writing (composition) portfolios, and some were about using portfolios to assess reading. None that we found dealt with the theory and applications of how to develop or create a portfolio and use it well.

The Purpose of the Book

The purpose of *So You Have to Have a Portfolio? A Teacher's Guide to Preparation and Presentation* is to offer universities, colleges, school districts, professors, teachers, and students a primer for portfolio preparation. The book may be used in professional development programs, teacher assessment programs, and teacher preparation courses. We have set a goal of fully defining portfolios, of giving the theory base for the various kinds of portfolios, and of showing how to collect data for an appropriate portfolio presentation. This theoretical and definitional material is contained in the first four chapters of the book which deal with an acronym we have coined *CORP*:

collection, organization, reflection, and presentation. The theoretical chapters deal with the importance of creativity in the collection, organization, reflection, and presentation of the assessment portfolio. They offer several tools for each of the processes and compare the portfolio process approach with the other disciplinary processes.

Besides the theory, we also have provided user forms, guidelines, protocols, sample rubrics, and other practical materials to make the portfolio a working document to show student growth or student accomplishment. The practical tools of the portfolio are contained in Chapters 5 through 8, where the practitioner will find samples, checklists, and other hands-on materials available for use in completing the portfolio project.

Who Will Be Able to Use the Book?

Those who will benefit from the text are educators who will be teaching the portfolio process to students compiling portfolios. Both of the authors have been teaching the portfolio process at East Central University in Ada, Oklahoma, over a combined period of several years, and we searched long and hard to find a single usable text for both the theory and the process. When we found none that we thought practical or useful enough, we decided to prepare one that could be used in our classes. We incorporate in it all the templates we have found useful in our teaching and assessment. Any teacher who deals with portfolios for assessment should find the book and its applications useful for their teaching. We hope that we have taken the fear out of the portfolio approach to assessment because we feel that the future will demand more individualized, sophisticated, and complex methods of documenting learning such as the portfolio process affords.

We certainly are not the originators of the portfolio in educational assessment, but both of us have used portfolios in our teaching experiences at both the elementary and secondary levels prior to our adding the dimension of teacher preparation as a level. We have tested the portfolio as an assessment tool with students at all three levels, but in addition, we have also used the materials in conducting workshops and presentations in state, regional, and national educational conferences. Our theories and tools have been examined by the participants at these conferences and have held their place well.

The theories and practical applications of the theories have proven useful to us by many years of applied success. We still use the materials in our classrooms and for presentations. We find that many schools ask us to bring teacher training seminars in portfolio assessment to their faculties. We share the materials with common school educators to make their program assessments more complete. We have expanded the idea to classrooms for students with special needs and have met with great interest on the part of special education teachers and their students who have successfully used the proposed process and CORP.

Brief Chapter Overviews

Chapter 1 deals with the definitions of a portfolio and details the thoughts behind the development of the portfolio as a tool of assessment. The chapter answers the following questions: What is a portfolio? What are the important factors that guide portfolio preparation? What is the difference between a portfolio and a scrapbook? Why do I need a portfolio? This chapter also discusses authenticity, ownership, and creativity in the preparation of the portfolio.

Chapter 2 details the developmental portfolio and its background as a tool for reflections about how one grows. Some of the questions answered by the chapter include the following questions: What constitutes a developmental portfolio? What makes this kind of portfolio useful? How is a developmental portfolio different from other kinds of portfolios? What kind of student would prepare a developmental portfolio?

Chapter 3 discusses the showcase portfolio, highlighting its uniqueness as a tool of success and self-esteem building. Some of the salient points of this chapter answer the following questions: What constitutes a showcase portfolio, making it unique? How does one select the "best" materials for use in the portfolio? When is a showcase portfolio more necessary than any other kind of portfolio?

Chapter 4 characterizes reflection as a heuristic device in self-examination. Reflection is the backbone of the portfolio. It helps one gain ownership of the plan and design of the portfolio. The chapter examines the following questions: How do I evaluate the artifacts that I have found for the portfolio? What does self-reflection do for the preparer and also for the audience of the portfolio? How do I make the reflections wholly mine and yet acceptable to the judging audience?

Chapter 5 is on the planning and organizational stages of the portfolio. It answers questions about what one must include in a portfolio and how the completed portfolio will look. The chapter examines the following questions: What do I have to include in the portfolio? What do I want to include? How should the completed portfolio look so that it truly reflects me? The chapter also presents various methods of organizing ideas and artifacts that will help the student be fully known to the evaluators.

Chapter 6 delineates the importance of the audience and how the portfolio will help its preparer in the real worlds of getting grades or getting jobs. The chapter helps the reader understand the following questions: Who will be looking at this collection? How can I tailor the portfolio to meet my needs? How will the portfolio address professional standards? How do I know which artifacts to include? The chapter discusses which materials are useful for obtaining a promotion, for faculty review, or for a capstone for graduation. It also attends to self-assessment tools as a part of the reflective process.

Chapter 7 contains the nuts and bolts of putting the work together and getting it ready for presentation to your desired audience. It answers the following questions: How do I assemble various portfolio components? What electronic sources are available to help me? How can I create an electronic portfolio? The chapter contains charts, forms, plans, protocols, and rubrics that will aid the preparer in completing the personalized self-awareness journey that concludes with the final copy of the portfolio.

Chapter 8 contains the details of the presentation of the portfolio to its audience. It answers the following questions: How do I prepare for an oral presentation? What questions are frequently asked during presentations and interviews? How do I integrate my portfolio during a presentation for job interviews? This chapter gives the portfolio owner insight and ideas for better presentation and communication.

This Book Should Meet Your Needs

We hope that the book meets your needs as well as it has ours. We have used these materials for several years, and they have been rewarding to us and helpful to our students. Our acronym, CORP, will help users of the material to more easily understand the process application. The portfolio can become a tool that will allow teachers at every level to see well-collected, suitably organized, appropriately reflected on, and well-presented (CORP) portfolios.

Acknowledgments

We appreciate the patience and help of many who have assisted in the writing of this book. We want to thank our families—children and grandchildren—but especially our spouses, Louise Wyatt and Benny Looper, for their encouragement during the creative process. Unless one has been through the process of writing a book, there is no way of understanding how much time has to be taken away from the normal operations associated with life and living. We have had discussions with our spouses, neglected them, asked comments from them, and complained to them of the aches and pains that creativity brings. They have stood beside us well, and for this we offer them special thanks.

We are thankful for the electronic highway that has carried messages through this year of writing. Although the Web and its technology ensnared us at times, it has illuminated and expedited the messages between Seattle and Ada. For reduced telephone bills we are grateful.

Our students deserve a nod of appreciation. For several years, even before we thought of writing such a book, our students have been our captive laboratory assistants for developing and trying new ideas. They have worked willingly, only complaining occasionally about the work and forms, and have made us aware of the needed changes in teaching strategies. Their feedback provided us the impetus for continued professional growth. We owe them a debt of gratitude.

We do appreciate our colleagues and their confidence in our ability to complete this project. Kenneth Moore, the dean of the Education Department at East Central University, has been most supportive and urged us to attempt this project. Having written three books himself, he knows about the time needed, and the thrills and exasperations of completing a text. Thanks, Ken.

Thanks also to those who pioneered the ideas and values of portfolio assessment. We have studied from, listened to, and read about so many and have adapted many of their ideas in crafting our own theories of portfolio development. We owe each of you a heartfelt thanks.

We appreciate Alice Foster of Corwin Press for her assistance and her faith in us. She contacted reviewers for our proposal, and we appreciate their feedback and ideas. For their contributions, the following reviewers are gratefully acknowledged: Paul Gathercoal, California Lutheran University, Thousand Oaks, California; Judith Brush Griffith, Wartburg College, Waverly, Iowa; and Nancy H. Phillips, Lynchburg College, Lynchburg, Virginia.

Without this kind of assistance, we might not have persevered. We hope the reader is pleased with the reflections and information found within these pages. They are truly the culmination of people, ideas, and personal philosophies.

About the Authors

Robert L. Wyatt III is Associate Professor of Education at East Central University in Ada, Oklahoma, where he has taught for the past 9 years. He also taught education courses as a graduate instructor at the University of Oklahoma while completing his doctorate. He previously taught at the secondary level in Texas, New Mexico, and Oklahoma for 25 years. He has led more than 100 workshops and seminars for staff development during the last 10 years. He has twice been named Teacher of Excellence at East Central, an honor that can only be awarded every 4 years and is usually nominated by students and elected by peer review.

Wyatt is a language arts specialist for both the elementary and secondary levels. He teaches undergraduate courses in methods for language arts; social studies (both elementary and secondary); clinicals I, II, and III; children's literature; young adult literature; and teaches graduate courses in modern philosophies of education and public relations for school administrators and librarians. Wyatt's previous book, *The History of the Haverstock Tent Show: The Show With a Million Friends*, was published in 1997 by Southern Illinois University Press.

In addition to his teaching, Wyatt is a selling artist of watercolor and oil paintings. He also has three novels out for publisher review, is a former owner/editor of a weekly newspaper, and is the author/publisher of three books of local history.

Sandra Looper is Adjunct Professor at North Seattle Community College in Seattle, Washington, in the Parent/Family Division. She currently teaches an on-line parent education class titled Special Topics for Parents of Young Children, and also provides independent consulting for various programs. She has been a presenter/speaker for more than 150 professional development programs with special interests in the areas of positive school climate, parent involvement, attitude/motivation, team building, technology, effective teaching, and portfolio development. She began an independent consulting business, Teaching From the Heart, in 1992, and is a certified trainer for On the Way to Success with Early Prevention of School Failure as well as an instructor for Parenting With Love and Logic.

An educator for 27 years, Looper has a B.S. in elementary education and an M.A. in counseling. She is certified as an elementary teacher, principal, and counselor, and has taught classes in the areas of school administration, early childhood and parent education, and curriculum and portfolio development. She recently served as Associate Director of an innovative elementary education program called Teachers Educating and Motivating Students (TEAMS), in which public school mentors and university students and faculty worked collaboratively to better prepare education students for the "real world" of teaching. She has presented numerous papers on the role of portfolios through the TEAMS Project as well as on the importance of mentoring. She has written articles for *The Teacher Educator, Principal, Connections in Education,* and *Learning* (pending publication).

1

Defining Portfolios and Their Purposes

Dr. Bryan and Dr. Green, both integral people to the education department's professional education division, look at a mandate from the state's educational governing body. They note that their professional education students have to prepare and be ready to exhibit what the report calls "a professional portfolio."

"I have heard of portfolios in art and in the stock markets, but what is a professional education portfolio?" Dr. Green asked.

"Maybe it is some kind of collection of professional papers such as résumés and letters of recommendation; or maybe it is just a collection of professional items. Isn't that what a portfolio is in the fields you have mentioned? I've heard of the writing classes requiring a portfolio, too. One of my students complained about having to keep up with everything that she had written in her English classes. Perhaps we can get information somewhere on what portfolios are," Dr. Bryan added.

"I just hope it is not just a new fad that someone has thought up for us to have to do in education. We have plenty to do now to get across the methods and pedagogies of education. We are required to do assessments of all that work already. This memo says that this is a part of our new state assessment plan for education," Dr. Green said.

Special buzzwords have been rampant in educational circles for the past few years. Terms such as *critical thinking, authenticity, hands-on, student centered, reflection,* and *qualitative assessment* have been right at the head of the list. But perhaps the most provocative among the buzzwords has been *portfolio.* Ironically, a portfolio can easily cover critical thinking, authenticity, hands-on, student centered, reflection, qualitative assessment, and more.

What Is a Portfolio?

An educational portfolio is a very personal collection of artifacts and reflections about one's accomplishments, learning, strengths, and best works. The collection is dynamic, ever-growing and ever-changing. It shows a student's growth, (developmental portfolio), best works (showcase portfolio), or total output (comprehensive portfolio). It is a tool for reflection on the items collected and must be approached from the point of view of the compiler, the owner of the materials in the collection, or from the point of view of an assessor, one who looks at and evaluates that compilation of materials. The key concepts in *portfolio* revolve around collection, organization, reflection, and presentation (CORP).

The materials in a portfolio may be used by the owner or the assessor as a ready reference showing in an organized way just what the compiler has done. It offers an authentic framework for judgments of the effects of the work done by the owner of the portfolio. It is a tool for evaluation by the owner in self-reflection or by a prospective or current supervisor of the work that has been done by the owner and is shown in the collection of materials. A portfolio is not a scrapbook, because the items in the portfolio have some kind of reflection as to why those items are included in the collection, but it is something like a scrapbook in its presentational style. If there is no reflection from the owner on the materials collected, the collection is merely a group of artifacts without form and purpose, making it nothing more than a scrapbook. The organization of the materials, then, with a special reflection about why the items in that collection were included, make the collection a portfolio. Without the reflection, the material is just a folder or a scrapbook, and though each has its place in collecting and presenting relevant materials, the portfolio has the special capability of being presented to and viewed by an observer or an audience, who then can make observations or assessments of the value of the collection of materials (purpose).

Some Background About Portfolios

Portfolios are not by any means some new phenomena. Artist's portfolios, stock portfolios, and real estate portfolios have been around for many years, and these kinds of portfolios are similar to the portfolios that have more recently been adopted in educational arenas as qualitative methods of assessing students' work. An educational portfolio has its own unique presentational style, but it is not unlike the other kinds of portfolios mentioned.

An artist's portfolio is a collection of the artist's work. The artworks may be presented in a kind of developmental chronology. This would show an artist's progress in art, moving from beginning work to current work. This type of organizational pattern for presentation can be equated to the *developmental* approach of an educational portfolio.

Alternatively, should the artist choose, the work presented in a portfolio may be a showcase of the artist's best works. Often, the artist will arrange the pieces in the portfolio to show what one thinks is the ascending order of the best work done. Or, the artist could select only a very few of the works from a full career and then explain to the audience viewing the portfolio why each piece earned its particular place in the portfolio's order. Either of these arrangements would represent something like the *showcase* portfolio in educational parlance.

Finally, the artist could present everything created since starting in the art field. The items in such a portfolio could be in an explainable order or they could be chaotically stashed in the portfolio folder. This would be something similar to what education calls the *comprehensive* portfolio.

The artist's choice of pieces is decided according to the audience and the purpose of the portfolio. Both are determinants in deciding how to present the artwork in the best possible light. The artist's audience may be one to whom the artwork is for sale, a prospective buyer of the art pieces. Perhaps the audience is an owner of a gallery whom the artist is trying to entice to display the artworks. The artist may be trying to impress an employer who needs art skills in advertising or display, and who is willing to pay for the artist's creative abilities. Whatever the audience or purpose, generally the artist compiles the items in some kind of presentational folder, but rarely does the artist reflect in writing on the pieces in the portfolio collection. Generally, the portfolio is merely the showing of artwork. Occasionally, the artist may have to reflect in some way about his or her collection in an oral presentation to justify the order or significance of the work so that it will be acceptable for display or ownership, whichever the purpose of the presentation happens to be. This type of reflection is comparable to the reflection on artifacts in an educational portfolio.

A stock portfolio also requires choice by the compiler of that portfolio. This collection may be a comprehensive listing of all the stocks owned by the compiler, displayed so that others may know what is owned. It may also be nothing more than a justified list of stocks to show the owner's ability to select good stocks. The first example would be a comprehensive stock portfolio, and the second may be considered something of a showcase or a developmental kind of portfolio for stocks. However, if the purpose of such a portfolio is to explain the items selected for the portfolio to a first-time stock purchaser, the portfolio could require some very definite kinds of explanation and reflection as to why a particular set of stocks were selected to work together as a business portfolio. These portfolios are similar in nature to the educational portfolio, but they may not be nearly as thorough or complete in the presentation because the audience of such portfolios may not need the collector's reflection about which stocks have been included in a portfolio.

The real estate portfolio is nothing more than a collection of real estate deeds to show which pieces of property the owner has acquired. There could have been some reflection on the owner's part when certain purchases were made to justify placing that material in a real estate portfolio, and this kind of portfolio would definitely be something akin to the comprehensive portfolio in education. The exception is that the real estate portfolio has no reflection by the owner about why the pieces of real estate are in the portfolio.

What About Educational Portfolios?

Whatever the kind of portfolio, the owner must be aware of and ready to show why the collection was made and why it is presented in a particular way. The educational portfolio is not too different from the previously described portfolios. In education, portfolios also have become tools for assessment. They may be used as an assessment to move the owner to a new level of education, or they may be used to promote the owner. They also may be used to show the growth or potential growth of the compiler. Items in the educational collections must have some kind of value to the owner and to the portfolio's audience. The compiler knows in advance who the audience is and has a clear-cut purpose in preparing the collection. The owner needs to justify the purpose of each artifact, telling why that artifact is included in the collection for the specific audience to whom the portfolio is addressed.

Historically, portfolios first made their entry into education in the art field, but early on, art portfolios in education were not unlike the regular art portfolio because they had no written reflections; they were merely a collection of artifacts. Artists compiled their works in a large carrying case so that they could show their pieces to others or look at their own collected pieces for their own benefit. Later, for assessment purposes, art students who turned in their portfolios for grades had to be very selective about which pieces they put into their portfolios, and they also had to write or narrate some kind of reflection about why the pieces were included in their collections.

Then came educational portfolios in the English/language arts field. Writing teachers had long been experiencing a terrific inundation of written paperwork to grade. Their writing students had to prepare a great deal of writing to assure their writing teacher, their parents, and the school districts that the students had met the levels of writing capabilities set as standards of an educated society that was being goaded by rapidly expanding, sophisticated technological advancements. The writing portfolio was introduced and became a huge success, most particularly with the overworked evaluator of the writing: the English teacher. Users of the writing portfolio system of grading touted it as a reliever of the burden of teachers having to read and mark carefully every paper their students wrote. These teachers began to see some light at the end of the overwhelming grading tunnel.

The writing teacher had, for several years before the development of the writing portfolio idea, already organized peer writing groups in which members had input into each others' writing pieces. The writing process had already gained prominence in writing classes. This writing process generally consisted of a five-stage program for students to follow in which they helped each other polish their work before the teacher saw the pieces for grading. This lightened some reading/grading problems, but it did not really reduce the load. It just postponed the papers coming into the teacher's hands until the peer group had already done some evaluation and made suggestions for improvement.

Various writing specialists have their own ideas about what goes into writing processes. Murray was among the earliest to say that writing was an identifiable process when in 1968, his book, *A Writer Teaches Writing: A Practical Method of Teaching Composition*, introduced the idea of *process*. He discussed the following seven skills: discovering a subject, sensing an audience, searching for specifics, creating a design, writing, criticizing, and rewriting.

Later, in the 1980s, writing teachers generally agreed that all writers, whether professional or amateur, proceeded through five stages, generally delineated as the following:

1. Prewriting (the stage in which the student collects and gathers material for a written paper on a chosen topic)

2. Drafting (a rough-draft document written after the student has collected sufficient data necessary for putting together the given piece)

3. Revising (a stage that requires the writer to examine the data and its first written presentation, changing anything that is erroneous or just does not sound good to the writer)

4. Editing (a stage after the writer has made desirable content changes that allows editorial corrections such as spelling, sentence construction, and so on to be made)

5. Sharing/publishing (the time when the writer of the piece is willing to allow others to read the written work)

Whatever the stages, English teachers were happy to see some pattern evolve because that allowed them to set up a system for assessing the written work by having a peer writing group help with the revising and editing stages. When written pieces came to the teacher for evaluations, they had already undergone some group evaluations, and the peer writers had suggested changes that otherwise would have required many hours of teacher-made observations. Peer writing groups made the process move smoothly by having students help each other correct writing errors involving both logic and mechanics. Writing improved. Apparently, English teachers were doing something right by having students work together.

But that still did not lighten the writing teachers' grading load enough. They needed further help because society still said that the American students were not improving enough to meet the demanded standards. In the late 1980s, writing portfolios grabbed the attention of writing teachers. This program allowed students to take some responsibility for their own writing pieces by having each student select which pieces the teacher would evaluate. The writing students generally either selected a showcase approach to show off their best works over a given period of time, or they chose a developmental approach to show their improvement in writing over a given period. Whichever approach the students chose, the teacher was thankful for no longer having to read and grade every piece of writing in their students' comprehensive portfolios of writing.

In either the showcase or development approach, once students gathered the materials, teachers could do a heuristic or holistic qualitative assessment of those items that each student had selected from their total works. Then, as a further device that allowed the teacher to know that the student knew why he or she selected the works presented for evaluation, a movement began requiring students to reflect on *why* they had chosen a limited number of pieces out of a large repertory of written work. Each had to do a reflection on why the items presented were chosen.

In cases where developmental ideals were sought, a student could tell in the reflection how the selected piece showed growth in skills. This could be done by presenting in the portfolio a progression of materials telling why the student thought the items chosen showed developmental growth and writer progress.

Or, the student showcasing written work could offer some kind of justification on the selection of showcase pieces for the presentational portfolio. This technique for assessment quickly caught on and proved to be substantially better for the English teacher, easing the grading load tremendously by not requiring teacher examination of students' total output of writing. The student writers felt authentic ownership of their own works, whether in a developmental or a showcase approach, getting some input on the pieces selected from trusted peers in the peer writing groups and perhaps letting parents in on the final selection process. Even if the teacher required (or was required by the school district) to see a comprehensive portfolio, the students could be asked to earmark those particular pieces that each wanted to be evaluated by the teacher. That would still give students a new idea of ownership of the material.

At present, the portfolio for assessment purposes is dominant at basically all levels of English education from early elementary through higher education. The English student and teacher are much happier with this authentic approach to assessment. Teachers feel that there is a greater sense of purpose in allowing students to choose those pieces with which they are most secure, or of which they are most proud. This pride of ownership seems to have made for better scores on standardized writing tests. Teachers are more satisfied that their grading loads have been lightened.

Because the English departments of schools have seen the potential of the portfolio, other discipline areas have picked up on the process. The portfolio has become a much praised system of assessment in most educational disciplines. Science has lab portfolios. Math has designed a portfolio approach for having authentic math-problem projects. Music allows students to perform pieces on audiotapes to show their developmental or showcase capabilities in their presentational skills. Technology has made possible interactive multimedia electronic portfolios.

In more recent years, higher education has gotten into the process and adopted the portfolio as an alternative method of assessment. Many colleges now require that a general education portfolio be submitted as an exit requirement from the general education section prior to one's getting totally involved in a specific discipline. Most of the disciplines, spurred on by assessment research or by the actions of various educational governing boards, are also adding some kind of portfolio requirement. In some states (Oklahoma, for example), students seeking certification in teaching at all levels and in all disciplines are being required to present a portfolio for completion of degrees in education leading to certification. In many instances, portfolios are being required at both the undergraduate and graduate levels. Furthermore, some districts require a portfolio for promotional and tenure purposes. Portfolios offer an organized approach to showing output of students, and they offer some proof that work has been done in given environments.

In some cases within the education discipline, even prospective school districts' employers ask that candidates bring in portfolios so that administrators and personnel directors may assess their works as a screening tool before the prospects are interviewed for a position in the school system. These employment portfolios are more or less of the showcase type (because some border on scrapbook presentations, especially those that are commercially presented in a scrapbook format). But however the document looks, the point is that now the teacher (or teacher prospect) as well as the student is faced with building a portfolio for assessment purposes, and the common education teacher is faced with preparing one for job retention, promotion, or tenure. Even in higher education, professors have to prepare and present a portfolio as an assessment tool in order to be promoted or to gain tenure in most colleges and universities.

The portfolio process is dynamic; that is, it is ever-growing and ongoing. The key to the process is not creativity, although creativity is extremely important and plays an important role in putting together a more palatable presentation. The real factor for assessment is the reflection. Reflection is a superior tool for presenting individuals and their work most effectively.

Is There a Process Approach to Portfolios?

The writing teacher spends time teaching the writing process. Though the stages of development vary, the final outcome of improved writing results from application of the process.

Each writing teacher adapts the process to his or her own philosophy of teaching. As long as the teacher and the student realize that the process is not linear, but recursive, it will work. *Linearity* simply means that one step logically follows another, and the second step cannot be taken until the first step is complete. In this instance, *recursive* means that from any stage in the process, the writer/presenter can jump back to a previous step or move forward to any step in the process as progress is made toward the presentational stage. Most creative work is by nature recursive and does not have a specific hierarchy for development.

We have developed a process approach to portfolios that should help the teacher and the student to understand the items that must be present for the portfolio to be complete, effective, and successful. The acronym CORP stands for our approach to portfolios. The letters in CORP represent the following operations in the portfolio process: collection of data, organization of data, reflection on the selected data, and presentation of the product. Just as in the writing process, the process is recursive. At any stage along the developmental lines, up until the presentation stage, the data may be changed, rethought, and adjusted. Those changing factors are what makes the portfolio dynamic rather than static. A scrapbook, for instance, would be static. The photographs and items in a scrapbook would likely all be chosen for the scrapbook for a specific purpose, and though they could be altered to change the mode of the approach to presentation with no reflection, they are virtually unchanging and sit still, without growth.

When students work on portfolios, on the other hand, they know that the material can and should be changed with the growth and reflection of the owners of the material. This approach does not, of course, mean that the preparer of a portfolio with a specific purpose and audience in mind can chaotically just jump around with the data. The very idea of a portfolio suggests an organized presentation of the preparer's works, thoughts, plans, and so forth. The document must be made with a clear-cut purpose and a definite audience in mind, just as is required in a writing portfolio. Some universities have ignored these facts in setting very rigid guidelines in portfolio development. One can still have organization without the direct linear approach that says, "I must include this, then I must do this, then I must show this." A portfolio cannot be prescribed that meticulously, or the preparer loses ownership, and the purpose of such a presentation is not clear to the preparer or the observer. One can choose any number of data, then limit the number from that expansive list, as long as there is the knowledge that each piece chosen must have a reflection to make it an authentic part of assessment. Or, the preparer may throw out all of those many pieces of data previously chosen and gather an altogether new set of data for the presentation, making new reflections as to the choices. One may repeat that process several times in the first stage of CORP, the collection stage. The portfolio can progress in that changeable manner all the way to the presentation stage of the portfolio, but the preparer might think of something else that should have been included to make the portfolio closer to completion. A recursive act can occur. The preparer can jump back and begin collecting new data even at that stage in the process. There is no need for linearity when one may recursively look again at the document and make changes at any stage of the CORP process. On the other hand, the preparer may have a plan so well mapped out that the process approaches linearity (some people are that meticulous in their own organizational techniques and can set their own prescriptions), but the owner will still use a great deal of creativity to present the items so as to make their inclusion in the portfolio justifiable to the audience and to the purpose of the specific portfolio.

What About Creativity?

Creativity is a very important part of any educational or life-enhancing pursuit. Creativity is definitely a part of the portfolio preparation and presentation, regardless of the portfolio's purpose or its author's learning/teaching discipline. In order to appropriately train a student in the creative processes, one should be aware of the stages of creativity. Goleman, Kaufman, and Ray (1992) list the five stages of creativity as preparation, frustration, incubation, illumination, and translation. Their approach to creativity is expanded linearity, also. The last stage must have all the other preceding stages in it, but otherwise the other stages are somewhat flexible. Once the creative being experiences the illumination stage—the "Eureka!" moment, when the light comes on in the darkness—there is less recursiveness because a definite end goal is in sight, but the illumination may cause one to become totally recursive to clarify his or her idea. Goleman et al. (1992) further state that the "act of creation is a long series of acts, with multiple and cascading preparations, frustrations, incubations, illuminations and translations into action" (p. 23).

Every person has certain thought processes that involve creativity. Gardner (1993) divides the various thought processes into eight categories that he refers to as "multiple intelligences." He has spent a great deal of time in written discussions and documentations of these various intelligences, and he ties creativity into each of them. He certainly advocates the importance of creativity as other authors have delineated it, but he himself has also written a book on creativity and the development of creative processes (Gardner, 1993). Gardner suggests that one can work in his or her own way to build a creative piece, and that when each works at an individual speed and thought process, though there is variety in the created pieces, there is a final creative piece that has some appeal across the thought patterns.

I may have one idea for the organization of my portfolio, and I may approach that idea with very creative, artistic artifacts because I am a writer and a visual artist. That would not mean that mathematically or scientifically oriented persons could not have the same quality of presentation of portfolio using that which appeals to them in pulling together their ideas for presentation. The difference would be, perhaps, in the portfolio's appearance, not in the kind of material presented. The way one sees and reflects on the artifacts would constitute the main difference in the portfolio's appearance. The artist would, perhaps, have an artistic flare in the artifactual presentation; the mathematician would, on the other hand, have a more logical approach in presenting the materials and reflecting on them. Both approaches would be acceptable, with neither presenter being right nor wrong. As long as a plan and the basic CORP approach is followed, the preparer is right because that preparer has to decide which artifacts best support the premise that the portfolio is trying to articulate.

Because the portfolio is now being required in many educational settings, some teachers or schools are making the portfolio, and what is to appear in it, very prescriptive and somewhat mechanical. For instance, some teachers state that all portfolios are required to have a specific folder/binder in which to present the information. Some teachers are giving the students a list of artifacts that must be included in the portfolio (transcript, letters of recommendation, videotapes, CD-ROMs, etc.; see Resource F). There would appear to be little creativity in this kind of required format/material, but the fact is that the creativity comes in the reflection that each student makes as to why a specific piece of documentation is included in a portfolio.

Questions arise to the preparer during reflection: Why did I choose the specific artifacts I have finally decided on for the portfolio? How does the artifact substantiate that which I am setting out to prove or support? Where does this piece fit into the scheme of the overall picture I am trying to present? Will my audience understand my choice of an artifact and my reflection on it? All of these questions are pertinent and all should be answered, but once the preparer is satisfied that the material is correctly done and adequately presents him or her, the portfolio becomes a documentary as well as a personal assessment tool.

Looking at the Portfolio as an Assessment Tool

Once the portfolio is agreed upon as a device of assessment, those involved with the portfolio need to reach an agreement as to what should be examined for the presentation. They need to decide whether the portfolio will be seen by peers, a teacher, a committee, and/or by a supervisor—in other words, who the audience will be. The audience is perhaps the most important single factor in setting up the prescription for a portfolio. When a teacher sees that a student needs to show improvement in a discipline, perhaps the best kind of portfolio would be a developmental portfolio. The teacher and the student would have a portfolio conference to determine the kinds of materials that would be of greatest benefit for evaluation. Though they would not select pieces together to use as artifacts in a specific portfolio, they would discuss the kinds of items that perhaps could be used in the portfolio. The preparer still feels ownership, yet the observer/assessor also has a responsibility in the process.

The coworking approach leads the preparer to know what the assessor would like to see in a portfolio, and also helps the preparer understand the process of evaluation and thus engage in a self-evaluation process. The reflection part of the process of portfolio preparation is really nothing more than a self-evaluation articulated in writing. Students evaluate artifacts they want included in their individual portfolios based on what they think the teacher has articulated for the assignment. The student still maintains authority and ownership over the work presented but knows more or less what is expected from the portfolio conference.

The portfolio conference may be worked through in a simulation in peer groups so that students may discuss among themselves what they think their instructors want. However, one of the important factors in portfolio preparation is that each of the students may be preparing a different kind of portfolio based on that individual's specific needs. That is one of the important factors in using portfolio assessment. Some students need to show progress, whereas others need to showcase best works. The portfolio is a very individualistic assessment tool that would be similar to a special education teacher's writing an Individualized Education Program (IEP) for each student in the special education classroom. That is one of most important factors in individualized assessments. Each student is evaluated based on that student's individual need. A teacher who uses that tool will find the successes and self-esteem building from making each portfolio an important project. This will indirectly cause the student to make more rapid progress toward an individualized goal.

The Role of Goal Setting in the Portfolio Process

Once students know that they will be evaluated on the artifacts and their reflections on each individual artifact, they will begin to realize that in order to reflect on a piece for presentation, they must have a goal in mind. If a teacher can point out the value of goal setting before the artifact is accumulated, the students will more effectively search for or prepare their artifacts for their portfolios. They must be instructed as to the purpose that a piece is to meet, whether the piece is a found piece of documentation for a specific competency, or whether it is a document or problem that the students themselves prepare. They must be aware of the *why* of an assignment. What teacher has not been asked, "Why do I have to do this assignment?" Using the portfolio approach will also help teachers assess the value of their assignments because they will need to know, themselves, why they assign a specific project, research paper, article, problem, physical activity, and so forth. The teacher's introspection about student assignments becomes valuable to both parties. Reflections make for better students. They also make for better teachers who are more aware of students' needs while they are collecting data for the first stage of the portfolio process.

Another important factor is that this approach to collecting data can be used for students at every capability or maturity level. The process and the assessment cause the goals to be differently set for each student preparing the portfolio. This has been effectively demonstrated at the secondary special education level, where students become exuberant in their collections and selections of the proper materials to substantiate their reaching specific goals that they, along with the teacher's and/or parent's help, have set. They can feel the same satisfaction in their presentations as those at the upward end of the capability stage. That is why the process is valuable for all to know and use.

It is beneficial to engage in assessment regularly. Once a goal has been set, gathering data to help show that goal has been achieved becomes important. But when one reflects on an artifact for substantiation of goal reaching, then the reflection is the most creative and important part of the assessment, not the collection of the artifact. However, one has to have a goal and an audience in mind when the process begins. If you know your audience and your goal, you will not stumble around in trying to achieve it.

An analogy to reaching goals in the portfolio process is planning a trip, and the analogy is one that can be effectively used in planning and presenting a portfolio conference. When planning a trip to a distant city, for instance, the traveler has to know what the purpose of the trip is and the amount of money and time that is available for the trip. If I were going to travel to New York City from Oklahoma City so that I could see three specific Broadway plays, for example, and I knew that I had only two evenings and one matinee time set aside to see these three shows, I would not plan to go to New York City via the leisurely route in an automobile—I would likely travel the most direct route. I also would set aside a specific amount of money for the tickets, lodging, and meals for the limited amount of time I would be in the city, and I would decide what I would wear and how I would move from place to place within the city. I also might have to justify to myself (reflect on) why I chose to do the trip in such a short time, how I would spend my money, and where I would stay in the city that would provide the greatest ease of getting to the various theaters showing the plays. I would be involved in setting goals (making the trip with its special limitations), reflecting on those goals, and accomplishing them for a presentation to my friends upon my return. This kind of goal-setting activity is similar to what needs to be done in the preparation of a portfolio.

Summary

A portfolio is an evaluative tool (whose parameters are decided on in advance) for presenting a person's developmental growth works, best works, or comprehensive works. The artifacts presented in a scrapbook fashion are each reflected on in written or verbal documentation, showing how the preparer has reached a specific goal with the presentation of the portfolio. Portfolios concentrate a student's work, giving the teacher/evaluator a chance to focus in on what the presenter wants that evaluator to see.

2

Developmental Portfolios
Documenting Personal Growth

Toshina Lambert has students with several levels of abilities in her classroom. She wants to show that her students are making progress and has adopted the showcase portfolio as her method. She wants each student to feel comfortable with the portfolio process, but she recognizes that the showcase portfolio is not the answer for all students. Her dilemma is that she only knows about the showcase portfolio, but she does not think it is working well for Celest and Sean whose educational plans are limited by IEPs. Celest cannot spell, and Sean is a poor reader. Neither of them can "shine" with a showcase portfolio. Ms. Lambert approaches her supervisor with her dilemma.

"Why don't you try the developmental portfolio?" her supervisor asks. "In that way you can allow each student, including Celest and Sean, to do the kind of portfolio that meets each individual need. Some should do a 'best works' showcase portfolio. Others should show progress in the work they have done. The progress-enhancing portfolio is called the developmental portfolio, which shows how a student has grown from the first lesson up until the present. I suspect that the developmental portfolio will be the best fit for Celest and Sean, but they will still be doing an individual portfolio."

What Is the Definition of a Developmental Portfolio?

A developmental portfolio is one that shows the growth and development of students as they progress from one learning stage to another. The developmental portfolio is, as are all other portfolios, designed to be an individual's case study, but instead of showcasing best works, it is the study of one's growth and development during a given period of time. Again, it is not a scrapbook in which there are no analyses and no definitive plan in mind,

13

with every artifact chaotically arranged in a binder or folder. Instead, it shows a progression of development moving from Point A upward toward Point B. The person preparing the portfolio reflects on each artifact, placing the artifacts in chronological order to show growth or maintenance of progress.

The developmental portfolio goes beyond the idea of showing "Who am I?" It takes the personality of the preparer and shows how that person develops through various phases of learning: "Who am I becoming?" This kind of portfolio is perhaps more difficult than the comprehensive portfolio because students must look at their total output, and from that output show some logical, sequential development, then be able to defend their logic in choosing that developmental order. It becomes cathartic to students because they have to look closely for points within their output to determine how they have grown and what routes their growth has taken. These portfolios are not quite as recursive as other types because they must show a hierarchical ordering of what the students have learned and accomplished. Of course, recursiveness is a part of choosing the hierarchy of the items, and preparers may go back and forth over which items should be chosen. So there is something recursive in the process of making their reflections define and show growth, but the recursiveness is not as evident as when one literally goes back and forth among the stages of the process. There is a definite linearity in just ordering items into a historical hierarchy. The question that each student must answer about the artifacts and reflections in this type of portfolio is "How does this piece show how I have grown in comparison with the earlier pieces that I have collected?" This type of portfolio is very reflective and retrospective in its nature.

What Is the Effect of
This Kind of Portfolio?

One of the most interesting factors with the developmental portfolio is that if students preparing such portfolios see growth for themselves, they can take a great deal of pride in the ownership of their work. They have given their observer/assessor evidence to prove that they have grown, a reinforcement in their own minds of what they have accomplished. If they have that reinforcement and have shown growth, then self-esteem builds and even the most developmentally slow student can show movement by showing improvement from piece to piece. In a developmental portfolio, the students demonstrate to their assessor that "I am making progress. I have proven that process by giving you the pattern of my progress!"

The developmental portfolio may show just the tiniest bit of growth, but knowing that even some growth has occurred is very supportive and comforting to the student. When the observer, especially if it is a teacher of the student, can see the growth, there is also a feeling of accomplishment on the observer's part for having had a hand in the process of development. Again, growth generates growth from the perspective of the preparer or the assessor of the developmental portfolio.

In a developmental portfolio, one student may be able to show strides of growth whereas another shows just faint glimmers, but there is a special built-in pride in seeing whatever amount of movement that is shown. The idea of movement is the prerequisite for the developmental portfolio. This kind of portfolio is dynamic because there is movement, and a portfolio of any kind is designed for the preparer to know that life is not static, but moving. So an assessment of a developmental portfolio would be of high ranking if any growth at all is shown and justified by the owner's reflections.

In a special education class, the developmental portfolio can be an extremely viable assessment tool. Reflections may be presented differently in these portfolios. Students who may not have writing capabilities, for instance, may reflect on their presented artifacts by demonstrating their reflections in some kind of oral fashion. There may be nothing more than just showing their joy at being able to choose their own artifacts to indicate that they are moving upward in their educational life.

What Kinds of Questions Might Be a Part of Developmental Portfolios?

In all portfolios, the preparer/student must have ownership of the work. Students' portfolios must reflect that ownership, and teachers can ensure this by allowing students to choose artifacts that they feel show their style of ownership. Developmental portfolios have to have the same sort of organization or pattern that any other portfolio would have.

As the preparer collects data for this kind of portfolio, a primary question is, "What did I learn during the time period this portfolio covers?" Students need to show their audience the struggle they have had in selecting the artifacts that demonstrate their growth. They have to glean information that would help them reflect on their struggles, and ask themselves, "What did I learn?"

In a very advanced class on how to build a portfolio, students were asked to show their developmental growth. Though all of the students were present in the classroom when the presentation was made on portfolios and their building, each student reflected on a new or different thought learned from the presentation. Their list was almost startling because each of them learned something different. The presenter of the material listed a set of objectives for the listeners to attain, and the students met the stated objectives, yet they grew developmentally in their own ways. They learned the objectives set by the instructor, but each gained the knowledge from a different perspective. Each had a different grasp. With their own unique answers to "What did I learn?," each had the makings for a good developmental portfolio. Individual growth is the most important factor in developmental collections and reflections.

How Does One Set Up Parameters for Such Collecting?

Because students are to be the owners of the material presented in the portfolios, they must be a part of the planning involved in choosing what kinds of documentation need to be in the portfolio. They also must be a part of establishing an evaluation protocol (rubric) for scoring or evaluating the portfolio. If they have ownership of both the portfolio and the rubric, they will be much more adept at showing how they have met the rubric's requirements.

So, one of the first things that should be done is to set up some kind of group discussion. The group should include mostly peers, but the teacher/evaluator should be part of initial groups. As a group, they must set down the criteria that is to be included in their portfolios. If the teacher is not a part of the initial planning group, the group should make a presentation of its plans so that the teacher can have input about the criteria expected from the groups. If the portfolio is to be owned by the students, they must be a part of rubric creation.

After parameters have been set, checklists should be made available so that the checking process is easy and thorough. The checklist is usually devised by the teacher after students have verbalized what they think should be covered in the assessment. Some institutions may be confined to state mandates or university-generated protocols in which the student has little input. Regardless, the checklist allows students to have a continuous appraisal of where they are in the portfolio-building process. They can keep the checklist in hand as they prepare their presentational portfolio, and the teacher can certainly use a portfolio checklist to substantiate ongoing preparation and growth.

Portfolio making is a holistic process for students because it involves the whole of their beings. Even something as simple as the students' getting up before their classes to discuss their portfolios' needs helps the students to become better developed. This gives all of the participants a chance to have a sense that they belong to a group. Speaking before a group and/or making audiotapes of presentations made throughout a semester could also make excellent artifacts for the presenters' portfolios. The possibilities for showing growth are limited only by a student's creative imagination. As we've noted previously, the keys to success with a portfolio are documentation and reflection. The basic premise is to give credence to one's achievements by showing "What and how I have learned."

McLaughlin and Vogt (1996) indirectly describe the developmental portfolio when they discuss schema-based learning development. They note that "learning takes place when new information is added to previously acquired knowledge" (p. 10). The developmental portfolio is the product that proves that learning has occurred. Teachers greatly influence what is learned by aiding the students who otherwise cannot make the connections about how much movement has occurred in their learning. The judgment about "What have I learned?" must lie fundamentally with the student, and part of that learning is the capacity to show what has been learned with artifacts and reflection.

The Process of Learning That Brings Good Assessment

When assessment takes place, there are certain perspectives that have to be understood. When students realize the possibilities for assessment, there is growth, and when there is growth that stems from some mild inquisitiveness or curiosity, there seems to be learning. Narrowing the concepts into something that can be measured can cause a great amount of difficulty for the preparer of the portfolio and the assessor of that work. An integrative approach to learning seems to require five stages of activity on the part of the learners. That process is still changing, but at present it appears that the five stages for acquisition and retention of knowledge are investigation, discussion, demonstration, writing, and construction. All of them should be performed by the student, not the teacher. If students accomplish these stages on their own, there is no logical way that they will not be able to perform adequately when asked to showcase their knowledge.

The Five Stages of Learning

The *investigation* period is the time for the learner to gather data. It is very similar to the collection stage of CORP in portfolio design. If the learners gather their own data and understand what they gather as they gather it, then the material collected by them will have a higher chance of being retained. Investigation includes such things as listening to teacher lectures, looking at resources in the library, reading textual material, and engaging in any other kind of activity for gleaning information and fortifying the mind of the student who is doing the investigation.

Discussion takes a different turn in this kind of student-oriented work. Discussion has often been characterized by the teacher's asking questions with the responses to the questions coming from the students. In this context, however, the idea is for the students to discuss in peer groups whatever information they have collected. Working together as peers in discussions of learning is the solidifying activity for the developmental portfolio. Generally, once a topic is announced by the teacher, peer groups are instantly formed, or existing peer groups begin to respond to the teacher's announcement of the subject. In portfolio peer groups, the group may move directly to the discussion of possible items from their investigations for portfolio inclusion. Indeed, if the portfolio group has five members, and if each student in the group shares information on collected artifacts, then there is really five times the amount of learning occurring. Furthermore, the student's verbalization of the material considered for inclusion in the developmental portfolio aids in retention.

The third activity slated for the peer group is a *demonstration* in some fashion of the material that the peer group has decided is relevant to the understanding of the competency or goal of the learning. Each member of the peer study groups will participate in some kind of demonstration of the material that the group deems relevant for the portfolio presentation. This presentation is a physical demonstration of what they feel is important. If the competency requires that they understand multicultural education, then the group may document such learning with a folk song they have recorded from another culture for inclusion as an artifact in their portfolio. They also may demonstrate their learning by showing photographs of the historical buildings in the town as part of a unit on local history in a lesson plan that they have taught in a clinical setting. Each person in a peer group should have a chance to validate the artifacts within the group. Surely, the quality of the developmental portfolio will be higher because group members have now investigated, discussed, and demonstrated a thorough understanding of the artifacts they have chosen. Even more important, all have had their learning reinforced by hearing several peers justify their collection of artifacts. The teacher may have to fill in some relevant details, but the teacher's load has been minimized, and the students' learning has been maximized. Though they realize that their teacher knows more, the material that students learn is often more palatable when it comes through the mouths of their peers, in their own language.

The fourth step in this learning process is the compositional or *writing* stage, the reflection. Remembering that these listed learning activities are not hierarchical, the students may opt to do the writing before they actually get up and demonstrate their learning. The point is that they have a fourth opportunity to show how much they know about the chosen artifacts, and if they share their writing with their peer group or the entire class group, they are getting a great deal more exposure to the subject. Certainly, such extra exposure will enhance their developmental capabilities.

After investigation, discussion, demonstration, and writing comes the final stage: construction. This is the tactile/visual stage for the learner. *Construction* requires that the preparer of the portfolio understand the process of the portfolio organization. Each student must know that he or she can construct something that shows his or her development through various stages of growth.

These five stages of learning go hand in hand with McLaughlin and Vogt's (1996) list of five possible ways that teacher learning may occur. They list "(1) learning about the innovative perspective, (2) choosing ideas that work in our context, (3) holding discussion with peers and administrators, (4) interacting with students to ensure the assessment system would be collaborative in nature, and (5) aligning the innovations with university grading policies" (p. 11).

The first two items listed above are closely related to the investigative process in the five-stage learning program we propose. The third situation goes well with the peer group discussion and demonstration of ideas. The fourth may be equated with the writing section previously discussed. The final step they list is equivalent to the construction of projects. Either set of learning devices will work well for anyone who is trying to get at real retentive thought accumulation. The first four stages represent the stages of CORP process, with the actual building of the portfolio as the construction phase of the five-part plan for learning.

The basic premise is that there must be a plan so that an assessment and/or an evaluation of each student may be conducted. The preparer of the portfolio must have a part in that process so that understanding and awareness of the usefulness of learning occur on a regular basis.

Questions of importance involving the developmental portfolio might include the following: "What does the portfolio show that I have learned?" and "Has my progress been adequate or must I concentrate on certain elements more fully to show my learning?" Keep in mind that the more open-ended an assignment is, the more difficult the assessment will be. Once the students get the concept of portfolios, then the task of constructing one will be a minimal process for them to accomplish. Once one has *process* in mind, the task does not seem nearly so formidable. Instead of placing emphasis on showcasing and showing only best works, teachers who require developmental portfolios look at the progress a student has made. According to the ability of the student, progress and long-term retention are perhaps best reflected in developmental portfolios.

The developmental portfolio must show personal ownership by the preparer, literacy development of the owner, and academic accomplishment (to some degree) of the participant. The portfolio is very personal within the parameters that the preparer and the audience have set together.

The portfolio is an archival collection of data and documentation. When the documentation is collected, time must be allotted for the student to work on keeping the material in an organized pattern that places the items in a chronology from worst to best. If this is not done in a classroom on a regular basis, the task of ordering will be so large that the student will be overly frustrated and learning will be hampered.

The culling process requires students to make decisions about which items may be placed in their portfolios. They cull from a large number of artifacts that they have collected and make each piece that they choose relevant. Often, those who make development portfolios bog down in this process. They will come to their audience and get the teacher or their peers to help them decide on the ordering process. In fact, they may get their peers to decide which pieces to use. As long as ownership is maintained and the documentation is authentic to the student preparing the portfolio, help from others is allowable. If the document starts to become more like another peer's presentation or more like the teacher's expectation, then the portfolio has lost its effectiveness.

The reflection part of the process is very difficult until the final product has been selected and turned in for evaluation. The reason for this difficulty is that the rationale that shows the importance or value of an artifact is what the developmental portfolio is about. The preparers have to know that if the guidelines for the portfolio require five artifacts and reflections on each of the five items, even after five initial items have been selected, these selections are not carved in stone. One may certainly change any documentation if a new or reconsidered document later seems to tell better or more appropriately the preparer's story. This is where the recursive process comes into play in developmental portfolios.

If some items are chosen as the ones to best show development, and another artifact appears that is better, students can negotiate with the assessor/teacher to include a new artifact or add another document to help tell the full developmental story. Paradoxically, one of the hazards is also one of the benefits of the developmental portfolio. Once the portfolio is presented and assessed, nothing prevents an individual from later adding new pieces to show further growth and development. The developmental portfolio has to continue to show growth to be correct and effective.

If one cannot reflect on the choices for the portfolio, then the selections made are not appropriate. The reflection is the component that empowers the owner of the portfolio. The choices for the portfolio should show something of the owner in diverse contexts. Artifacts and reflections from outside the school participation context (i.e., other than tests, papers, book reports, etc.) would certainly offer some satisfaction to the assessor. If an artifact or a reflection does not empower the preparer and establish pride in the work, the owner should reconsider the effort involved and choose some other kind of artifact. A big success factor is making sure the task of compilation does not become so overwhelming that it cannot be accomplished. The teacher/facilitator must emphasize time-management skills so that time issues will not become a factor in the success and self-esteem flow of the student preparing the portfolio.

Summary

The developmental portfolio is a very useful tool for checking the progress of the preparer from the preparer's point of view. Artifacts for the portfolio are selected and then reflected on by the preparer. The artifacts must show progression in a hierarchical order ascending toward the best work of the preparer. There must be evidence that some special selection has taken place to assure that progress is shown. This portfolio works for any capability level; even though the last artifact may be among the best works of the presenter, that work may not be "good" in comparison with others who might be presenting another type of portfolio. The work shown should indicate that the presenter has moved upward, progressed. *Progress*, then, is the key word for assessment in this kind of portfolio work because the one preparing the portfolio can justify growth through the reflective pieces that accompany the artifacts. This portfolio will have an entirely different rubric from the showcase or the comprehensive portfolio. Students preparing the developmental portfolio will help the evaluator decide which items will be assessed by the rubric and how they will be assessed. In fact, each portfolio will basically be judged on the assumption that progress is made, and the criteria for the assessment will simply ask if progress has been shown from the first to the final artifact.

3

Showcase Portfolios
Putting Your Best Foot Forward

"I want to show you my work, Dr. Rodriquez, but I do not want to show you everything I have done, and I don't want to put the things that I think are my better pieces into a somewhat chronological order. I just want you to see what I have to offer. What should I do?"

"What you are asking about is the showcase portfolio. You want to place five or six of your best pieces of work into a special collection for me so that I don't have to filter through all the pieces you have done this semester and perhaps miss those things you feel you are more accomplished in. Right?"

"That's it! Can I do that for you, and make sure you get my best stuff?" Sarah asked.

"When you choose your best works to show for assessment, we call that collection a 'Showcase Portfolio,' " Dr. Rodriquez said, "and the showcase pieces are chosen by either just you or both you and me. We can look through your comprehensive collection folder and choose just those representative pieces that you want me to evaluate for your semester's mark. You will, of course, have the final say in choosing the pieces you wish to be judged, and then you will reflect on why you made the choices you made. And that showcase collection is what I will mark."

What Is the Definition of the Showcase Portfolio?

As with the other portfolios previously discussed, the showcase portfolio is a collection of works selected by the owner of the portfolio for display. The very word *showcase* gives away the definition. This portfolio is the place wherein the owner can show off the works or pieces that set the owner apart from other preparers of portfolios based on the same general theme. The showcase is much like a glass display case in a museum or in a department store where objects are on display for special viewing or specialized sales. The showcase portfolio is in the same category. The pieces (objects) that are in the portfolio (display case) must have a special viewing (by a professor judging the student's work, by an assessment team making an evaluation of a program, or by a school official who views the portfolio with the idea of hiring its preparer).

What Constitutes "Best" Works?

The person presenting the showcase portfolio has to be astute in making judgments about the best works from a generally large number of selectable possibilities. One of the primary questions that the presenter has to ask is, "Who is the audience for this portfolio, and how do I best impress that audience with the selections I make for the presentation?"

One's showcase artifacts can change as often as needed to impress different audiences for different purposes. Because the showcase is changeable based on the needs of specific audiences, one is required to keep all pertinent materials that have been collected as possible display items in a comprehensive file so that from the comprehensive collection, appropriate showcase items can be selected and made ready for the specialized display. A teacher or a professor involved in helping the student get materials ready for a showcase presentation should ask the students who are preparing such portfolios to verbalize or, perhaps, to write a theoretical basis for the item prepared. At the same time, a written reflection as to why the piece needs to be included within a portfolio should also be prepared. By keeping materials and reflections in good order and current, a showcase portfolio may be pulled together easily for differing audiences and on very short notice.

The showcase, then, certainly does not negate the need for a comprehensive collection and constant reflection and justification processes, as one might think a showcase would. In fact, because the showcase does not rank pieces in the collection as does the development portfolio, one can randomly pull best works for this kind of portfolio. The presenter of the showcase portfolio would want no ranking—even a partial, unplanned ranking—because the presenter wants the reviewer to make judgments based on the overall coverage presented in the document and does not want to portray even the possibility of a growth pattern. The showcaser has already dealt with growth and wants the audience to know that what is displayed are the very best works the presenter has to offer.

What Are Problems for the Showcase?

Because the showcase is supposed to offer examples of a presenter's best works, the responsibility for selling the presenter lies fully in that presenter's court. The presenter cannot include pieces that could possibly disqualify, nullify, or in any way weaken or discredit the work shown. There has to be a great deal of soul searching as to which pieces, among many that are possibly available, will best tell the appropriate story for the presenter. When one is trying to determine those "best" works, one has to rely on his or her own judgment to make qualified decisions that will please the audience. The showcase portfolio could easily be the most difficult kind of portfolio to prepare because of that big decision factor. The preparer has to do some astute audience and purpose analysis to decide which items are appropriate and best works for such a portfolio. The ideas of *audience appeal* and *audience pleaser* certainly come into play more with the showcase portfolio than with any of the other kinds. The preparations must show a high level of confidence that the right choices have been made for the portfolio collection. One still has to move through the CORP steps and still must spend a great deal of time in reflection. And because this portfolio shows only one's best works, the reflection process requires greater depth and perception.

How Do I Select "Best" Works for Presentation?

A main prerequisite for any kind of portfolio is the collection process—the *C* of the CORP process. The preparer should collect every kind of artifact that would enhance a portfolio. Very often this material turns out to be something that is not usable, but the preparer must remember that if one is trying to show best works, he or she must choose different artifacts than when one is seeking to show growth or development.

From the collected materials, then, and without considering the hierarchical arrangement of the materials, the preparer has to make evaluative judgments of the artifacts, selecting those that best meet the needs of the audience who will view the works. A good knowledge of the audience selected to see the portfolio is a necessity when one is approaching a showcase portfolio. The materials in a showcase portfolio are meant to tell the world that the preparer is the best specimen available to the addressed world. The way that the material is shown should emphasize that best-specimen image. Therefore, one of the most important factors in the showcase portfolio presentation is the selection of the works for the portfolio.

The showcase portfolio should also certainly be a dynamic work, with the strongest emphasis on *dynamic*. This kind of portfolio is not one that the preparer can put together and then sit back and relax with the attitude that "Whew, this is done now. All I have to do is present it over and again." The artifacts for the collection can change as frequently as one collects new artifacts. Even in developmental kind of growth, as one progresses the work should improve with each piece of documentation that one prepares. The developmental portfolio is more logically set and static than the showcase. If one is trying always to show best works, then the showcase should be updated as often as new, superior work is done. The materials become an ever-changing exhibit owned by the preparer and presenter of the portfolio. When one is showing his or her best side, better, newer materials should be added as often as the opportunity arises.

The showcase collection is carefully designed to reveal achievement. Achievement is the key to the success of the collector, and evaluation of the showcase is generally based on how well the preparer shows that achievement. If one seeks to prove competency in a given field, the pieces that best reveal the achievement of that competency would certainly be the documentation that one would choose for the showcase portfolio.

The evaluator of the showcase, the portfolio's selected audience, needs to feel an immediate impact of the value of the presenter. Good workmanship on the assembly of the documentation will certainly set up a good first impression of the presentation. A sense of good organization and planning for what goes into one's showcase must be obvious from the first opening of the portfolio.

Should Showcase Portfolios All Look Alike?

People know that traditionally those who make the loudest appeal get heard more quickly. That same approach surfaces, of course, in portfolios. Those who put the most glitz into the portfolio's design make their work glitter most, and that glitter attracts the quickest attention. So, a new trend seems to be developing among educators to keep portfolios similar in design within a given area or a given institution to keep one portfolio from standing out more than another. The thinking is that through this similar-look approach, each student is given a chance to have the work seen in its best light. Proponents of the uniform presentation approach would argue that having all portfolios look alike on the outside helps preserve equality and fairness in competition for recognition among the preparers.

In school situations, this attitude may be appropriate for those who have to evaluate many portfolios because they will not have to sift through mounds of fluff to get to the basic reason for the portfolio's creation. Most schools that require portfolios are asking for a showcase portfolio with a best-works emphasis, and if the presentation folders of the portfolios all look uniform, the argument that it results in better and more fair evaluation of the contents of the portfolio may be true because it is the content that is being appraised. But when a professional person, whether artist, teacher, or stockbroker, presents a showcase of work, there is also the argument that the presenter's personality should be a part of the presentation. That extra "fluff" makes that presenter stand out above the others who are in competition for the position that is open, for the sale of the portfolio's artwork, or for the promotion. Advocates of individualized portfolios suggest that after all, the real reason for the portfolio in the first place is to show off one's best efforts.

Those asking that the covers and divisional pages of the portfolio be uniform indicate that the choice of materials to be presented and the reflections on those materials—the contents—are the only items on which the presenter should be judged. Such a generalization is somewhat true, but for a showcase to be showcase, even the cover and the presentational style should perhaps reflect the "best works" idea of the presenter. Some folders, binders, or other presentational materials will appear to be overly creative, whereas others will be rather staid and vanilla. They are all passable and good if they meet the protocol set up by the preparer. The point is that the person preparing the portfolio is best represented by being able to choose the style in which his or her materials are presented. The personality of the presenter should definitely shine forth from the very first impression of the portfolio, and the first impression is usually the cover or the binder of the portfolio if it is presented in a book format. If uniformity conditions prohibit the presenter from being authentically represented, then perhaps the showcase idea of a portfolio has not been achieved. It is true that a certain level of craftsmanship and an appropriate professionalism should show through, but creativity must not be stifled in the process of trying to set uniformity standards for all the portfolios.

An argument for uniformity is that those judging the portfolios will not be distracted by anything extraneous, and can focus on just the contents of the collection if all the pages have a similar form and if the cover of the portfolio and the division pages are uniform. The judge's job may be easier if the protocol for the collection and presentation is more strictly set and adhered to. Those in classrooms or programs who prepare portfolios do move at approximately the same speed over their classwork. They use the same textbooks, take the same examinations, abide by the same set of rules; therefore, logic would argue that they should all use the same protocol and consistency in the way their materials are presented. A uniform rubric for how the portfolio is to be presented, then, would be adopted and used in the judging of all the portfolios. Proponents of the consistency idea argue that the portfolios should then be easier to evaluate, and that all will be judged alike.

Of course, once the showcase portfolio has been selected as the appropriate form of presentation, each individual prepares the document in such a way as to show ownership. Creativity shows up in a creative person's work—including portfolio presentation—almost unintentionally whether the presentation is in a uniform format or not. The very purpose of showcase portfolios is to show off one's creativity, and there is really little one can do to keep from letting that creativity show.

Another point about consistency is the fact that with the technology that is now available, each preparer can design and collect materials and record them on compact disks (CDs), an option that up until recent developments in manufacturing and marketing has not been feasible. Today the cost of a CD recorder is such that most schools can now afford to have one available, and even some individuals own the machines as a part of their personal computer tools. This CD recording process allows for a much wider choice of materials that can be presented in a limited space or limited collection. Many schools of education are requiring students to have on their CDs photographs of themselves in action in the classrooms. Many ask that students put videotapes of their teaching assignments and classroom presentations on the disk portfolio so that evaluators will have a more complete record of the student's activities as a preparing teacher. CDs are very easily catalogued and stored for a permanent record.

One of the problems with the electronic portfolio is that collectors tend to want to save everything on disk, and the evaluation becomes more of a comprehensive portfolio instead of the showcase variety. When one can save everything in such a small amount of space, best-works data is much more difficult to define and choose for showcasing. Most people, especially those who are unsure of what evaluators want to see, will tend to be too ready to save and share everything they have collected. When this happens, the portfolios stop being showcase presentations and revert to a comprehensive collection.

Why Would I Make a Showcase Portfolio as an Evaluative Tool?

There is not one among us who does not want to impress others, especially those who are in a position to give out rewards. The preparer of a showcase portfolio is in the same situation. If we look for jobs, or want raises and promotions, or strive for higher marks in the school record books as an evaluation of works done, the best promotion that can be accomplished is to show ourselves and our works from the best possible vantage point. This kind of promotion of our lives makes it appear as if we are preserving for posterity those good works that will reflect us for ages to come. All people want to have monumental histories written so that the world will recognize their worth after they have departed this life. The showcase portfolio is comparable to a monumental history of one's life over a given period of time. From that showcase, the preparer hopes that those appraising his or her showcase portfolio will be able to see that he or she deserves the best possible rewards based on this collection of artifacts and reflections about the works shown. All people want to reap the benefits of work well done. Whether we like to admit it or not, all of us would like to have a monument of some kind erected to our work, our creativity, and our memories. The showcase portfolio is at least the first step toward that monument's creation.

Gathering data and material is not an easy endeavor on its own, but choosing which material one wants to include as part of a monumental history is perhaps the most difficult part of the task. Another difficult area is telling the reviewer of the document (reflecting on the materials selected) why one believes the artifacts have achieved monumental status in preserving and presenting one's story appropriately and adequately to accomplish the desired results. Campbell, Cignetti, Melenyzer, Nettles, and Wyman (1997) suggest that a showcase portfolio presentation will be unique in "reflecting your abilities, your strengths, your professionalism" (p. 67). They suggest that the preparer should keep the presentation simple and straightforward because the presenter does not want to "detract from the work you are trying to showcase, nor do you want to appear as if you are hiding incompetence" (p. 16) by the way the material is presented. The basic idea of this kind of work is to show yourself to your best advantage so that others will admire you, hire you, or give you other considerations that you desire while still reflecting your autonomous self. Again, the preparer makes, through the preparation and presentation of the artifacts and reflections in the portfolio, a statement saying, "Here is what I have done," giving the chosen audience a full picture of what good things have been accomplished. The presentation becomes a show-and-tell about the owner's best abilities to meet the expectations of the audience. One must be sure that the showcase has not only good visual appeal, but also well-displayed substance.

Summary

The showcase portfolio takes more work than the other kinds of portfolios because there is a need to be very selective about what one puts into the portfolio. Those who prepare the showcase portfolio are individuals who have some special-type items to share, and who also realize that they have a special kind of audience with whom they strive so hard to share their carefully collected materials. The portfolio preparer must take care to present the material in a way that will place him or her in the best light for those viewing the work. There is no hierarchy of placement of materials, as long as where they are places them in position for the judgment of their work to be thorough and pleasing to their audiences. One must have a goal in mind so that when the portfolio is complete, one's best works shine forth.

4

Reflecting on Your Artifacts

"I understand your frustration about assessing your own work. It is difficult to do, but self-assessment is the first step in getting assurance that your portfolio is good," said Professor Pollard. "You have to do a self-evaluation or self-examination. I cannot make judgments for you as to why you chose the pieces that you chose. I can tell you whether or not I think the pieces are good work. I can tell you whether I think the pieces meet the obligations that we have agreed on for the assignment for the portfolio, but I cannot tell why you chose them."

"But who am I to make this kind of decision? I am just making preparations to teach. I haven't done it yet. How do I know which pieces make the best statement as to the competency that I seek to prove in my collection?" Tom Fuller, a senior in professional education, asked.

"Tom, I can give you a paper-and-pencil test, and that is one kind of assessment. For that kind of assessment you can memorize answers and parrot them back as you think I want to hear them. But it is your reflection and your heuristic evaluation that I really want to see. My judgment on what you have selected to prove the ownership of the competency is not nearly so relevant as why you think it proves the competency," Professor Pollard replied.

The Importance of Self-Examination in Portfolio Building

Ownership of the portfolio is one of the most important facets of the CORP process. The reflective stage is the ownership stage. Without this reflection, a portfolio is nothing more than a glorified scrapbook. Scrapbooks lack the kind of organization and presentation that allow for assessment of an

29

individual. The reflective part of the portfolio process, wherein the preparer asks and answers the question, "Why did I include these artifacts in my portfolio?" is the part of the process that allows for assessment. McLaughlin and Vogt (1996) note that the reflective process "encourages the students to ponder what course goals mean and contemplate their ownership of the portfolio process" (p. 33). This reflective section of the process is the part that makes the exercise authentic to the preparer of the portfolio. It establishes the value of the effort that is made in putting the work together.

Reflection is a part of life's regular routines. Not a day, not even an hour, goes by when there is no reflection about our daily routines and our experiences and circumstances. When we purchase an item that is an unusual operating expense and outside our budgets, there has to be a time of reflection on what the expenditure will do to our lives and our lifestyles. This meditation and contemplation about exceeding a budget or overextending a credit card, for instance, causes many people to go almost into a tailspin of reflection.

In another form of reflection, we constantly evaluate our stances on public issues in our desire to be more acceptable to a greater number of people. We meditate on whom we should vote for, what causes we should back, and where we stand. Reflection takes up a good bit of our time in our daily routines, and reflection holds us in line with our convictions and keeps us from being too spontaneous or impulsive. Reflection requires thought that borders on meditation.

What Is Heuristic Reflection?

Heuristic reflection, in the context of portfolio preparation, takes place when the owner of the artifacts reflects in a very personal manner (very subjectively) about why a specific item was chosen, and why it fits a particular need. The subjectivity of the owner is the key factor. Adorno (1989), interpreting Kierkegaard, calls this state "inductive subjectivity" and discusses the search for truth in the inward person. Those who own must "feel their own experience" (Morris, 1969, p. 138). This indicates that the owners of the portfolio materials must first select items that they feel meet the criteria they have set, and they must then reflect their own hypotheses, assumptions, and constraints from their own perspectives (Michalski, 1987). Habermas (1985) argues that inductive subjectivity is valuable for making choices and is ranked equally with scientific thought. Such choices, suggesting reflection, are then valid for portfolio reflection in helping the adjudicators approve the collections within a portfolio and in assuring the owner that what has been chosen is good as long as the chooser knows why the item was chosen and can reflect on and justify that choice for the collection.

Heuristic choice and reflection is a way of knowing that what has been done is acceptable. It "encourages an individual to discover, and . . . to investigate further" (Moustakas, 1981, p. 207). The discovery process is a definite part of this collection and reflection section for portfolio making. Individuals are ultimately responsible for their acquired knowledge. They must be involved in critical thinking to be able to justify their choices and the reflections they have made as a part of their record. The record is the reason for the existence of a portfolio.

Owners must be able to put their works into some kind of context after they have analyzed their audiences and after they know the approach they will take in the production of their portfolios. A developmental portfolio is very different in appearance and stance from a showcase portfolio or a comprehensive portfolio. Because they are different, they have different choices involved in their reflections.

Before a preparer can collate a portfolio, he or she must look at the whole picture, making the portfolio not only heuristically but also holistically approached. Individual pieces are chosen and reflected on because of how they lie within the whole picture that the owner wishes to produce. The preparer needs to combine and test combinations chosen for the portfolio, weighing them against one another to ascertain whether those items chosen truly reflect the bigger picture the owner wants to reflect. Heuristic reflection suggests a kind of intuitive reasoning as to which pieces to include in a portfolio document. Because the portfolio is a dynamic document, this heuristic approach is not foolproof, but the owner of the portfolio does not have to worry about foolproof selection. The document can and must change based on the needs of the owner to best portray his or her needs and goals.

How Do I Know If the Choices and Reflections Are Accurate?

McLaughlin and Vogt (1996) note that to internalize learning, reflection is essential. This is part of the process of learning to make judgments about which things are acceptable, which are not acceptable, and why they are such. Reflection helps one perform better in the future.

Self-reflection is a part of growth, indicating a maturity in making selections about one's own life. Then, learning becomes a process and reflection on the items collected in the learning process, and the sharing of those items aids in making a person more aware of who they are and how they became who they are.

When a document is chosen for the portfolio and is reflected on, then who is to argue about the validity of that piece of work being used in a portfolio? If one chooses a photograph, a newspaper article, a lesson plan, or whatever is needed to show either growth or best works, and can justify the use of that item in the proper sequence of putting a portfolio together, there is generally no way that any appraiser can set aside those arguments. No one judging the work can help but state that the items chosen are adequate or competent as long as the preparer knows what was chosen and why it was chosen for the portfolio. The next section shows an example and critique of a student's reflection on a specific competency.

Student Reflection on Competency 12

Competency 12

The teacher understands the process of continuous lifelong learning, the concept of making learning enjoyable, and the need for a willingness to change when the change leads to greater student learning and development.

Student Reflection

The student used a lesson plan as her artifact for substantiating Competency 12. The lesson plan dealt with giving two children a quarter each with which they could buy a tin of candy. One tin had 15 pieces and the other had 5 pieces. The question asked was, "Did the children get equal value for their money?"

The student reflected: "The concept of *lifelong* was addressed because in real life we often have to make choices with little more information than the amounts presented in the math lesson. Having the candy and the quarters made the learning fun and enjoyable for the learners and for me. From my foundations class lectures, I learned that it was important to reach children with both mental and physical activities. I believe that the lesson did both of these things" (Evans, 1997).

Critique of Student Reflection

Although the student addressed the concepts of *lifelong learning* and making learning enjoyable, she did not note the need for a willingness to change when change leads to greater student learning and development. She provided few details supporting her understanding of the competency.

The evaluators felt that this reflection did not meet an acceptable level based on the assessment rubric. As evaluators, we would recommend to the student that she should consider whether this particular lesson plan was the best evidence supporting Competency 12. We would also encourage her to use greater detail in documenting the student experience. Even though the evaluators could tell from the lesson plan and her oral explanation that further details were available to strengthen her reflection, she did not include those items in her written work. They suggested that a rewrite of that reflection would be valuable. The evaluators also suggested that some artifact must reflect the other component of Competency 12, the need for a willingness to change.

Summary

As the owner of a portfolio, you are the person responsible for making choices as to what will go into the portfolio. Inductive subjectivity makes both the choices and the reflection truly your work. As long as what you choose is justifiable to meet the needs of the judges, and as long as the artifacts are pertinent to your application of knowledge, you make the decisions as to what is included.

5

Mapping Out the Plan

Jamie was relieved to have reached the point finally where he was taking his professional teacher education courses. During the first day, as professors began to explain their course assignments, he kept hearing, "You may want to include this in your portfolio" and the words "artifacts" and "rubrics." It seemed that each of his classes was going to require many assignments, some of which might be used for this thing called a "portfolio," but as yet, no one had explained exactly how these things were going to come together. They talked about documenting clinical experiences, writing philosophies, even recording recreational and volunteer activities.

Jamie was confused. He wondered how past experiences, present activities, and future goals could ever be compiled into one document. How was he ever going to decide what to include? How much time was he going to have to spend getting this information together? He hoped that someone would explain exactly how he should go about planning and organizing this portfolio. Because he had never seen one, how was he going to create one?

Portfolios Are Diverse

Portfolios, like people, are very diverse. Some communicate information by being straightforward, cut-and-dried, to the point, concise, and abbreviated. Others are expressive, detail oriented, comprehensive, and lengthy. Because each portfolio is unique, the formula for planning portfolios must be universal, yet individualized; simple, yet complex; orderly, yet flexible.

Portfolios reflect not only what the institution mandates as important, but they also allow each individual to take the portfolio clay and mold it into something uniquely fitting that person. An initial question must be asked such as, "How is this portfolio going to be used?" or "What is the portfolio's purpose?"

Determination of Purpose

Before compiling information, it is vital to develop a clear understanding of the intended use of the portfolio. The purpose, more than any other factor, will drive the content and organization of the document. Some common reasons portfolios are developed include the following:

- For self-reflection to show growth and development over a period of time
- To showcase best work
- To provide prospective employers information about job skills
- To determine whether program goals or certification requirements have been met

Once the purpose has been established, the next planning phase can begin. When deciding what to include in the portfolio, one must ask, "What do I have to include in this document?" If a portfolio is being developed to meet class or program requirements, then there will be specific items that are mandated for inclusion. The student may have a great deal of latitude or very little.

Required Items

Some institutions require a very structured and sequential list of portfolio items, whereas others allow greater flexibility. Often, a generic form is presented to the entire student body and each departmental discipline develops its own criteria for the portfolio. Others schools of thought require that the portfolio be centered on students' understanding of competencies, and they want verification of knowledge of those competencies (see Resource B).

The National Board for Professional Teaching Standards (NBPTS, 1998), for example, requires very specific assessment items that allow teachers to present samples of their classroom practice over a specified time period. The early childhood/generalist must include five portfolio entries with the following general headings:

1. *Introduction to Your Classroom Community:* Teachers must show time and classroom management skills as well as a written commentary and a videotape.
2. *Reflecting on Teaching and Learning Sequence:* Teachers submit a written commentary and artifacts that demonstrate children's growth and learning within a theme drawn from at least two content areas.
3. *Engaging Children in Science Learning:* Teachers are asked to highlight an investigation of a science concept. Written commentaries as well as a videotape segment are to be included.

4. *Examining a Child's Literacy Development:* Teachers are asked to present ways in which they foster literacy development in their classroom. Student work samples and steps they would take to support the child's literacy growth, as well as a written commentary, are to be included.

5. *Documented Accomplishments:* Teachers are to document work outside the classroom with families and in the profession. Two summaries, including one for accomplishments with families and one for accomplishments in the profession, are required.

Common Components

Researchers have indicated several essential features of a teaching portfolio. Their lists indicate that a portfolio collection should be purposeful, selective, diverse, ongoing, reflective, and collaborative. The artifacts generally are structured around professional standards and individual/university goals. Each of the standards may have several indicators of demonstrated competencies.

The competency, indicator/indicators, captions, and written commentary should accompany each portfolio artifact so the reader understands why the artifact was included. Assuming a reader will make the connection between the artifact and the competency is risky. For example, students must clearly communicate why a picture of a bulletin board is included in the portfolio. Does it demonstrate a philosophy of student-centered classrooms? Does it reflect the importance of a stimulating, interactive environment? Does the bulletin board manifest the across-the-curriculum strategy linking math and science? Students need to inform the reader why the particular document is included by justifying the standard.

The following is a summary of East Central University student Terry Sanders' (1997) opening statement in support of a media technology requirement:

I have chosen to demonstrate my competency in media technology because I have gained quite a bit of knowledge in this area that will prove invaluable as a teacher. I've learned how to operate a photocopier that shrinks and enlarges. Having the copier available at my home has allowed me to share copies with friends and for emergency times during my student teaching.

I consider myself computer literate, having purchased a personal computer 5 years ago and 3 years later adding a second computer with a CD-ROM. The following programs are available to me: Grolier Encyclopedia, On the Menu Cookworks, Desktop Magic: The Ultimate Clip-Art Library, U.S. World Atlas, World Atlas, My Family Tree, and a Greetings Workshop.

In January 1996, I purchased a modem and went "on-line." We have full access to the Internet and e-mail. I have used e-mail to contact professors, friends, and family as well as other educators across the United States. The Internet has provided many areas of research during my college career as well as aided me in compiling many different lesson plans for future use. A word search program was purchased and an electronic grade book program has been downloaded. I've learned many instructional uses for the computer and the Internet.

I am proficient in Corel Word Perfect and was coeditor of a student newsletter. Currently, I've collected 11 disks of graphics; many of those downloaded from the Internet.

To document the previously mentioned information, I've included samples of papers done using the computer, e-mail, and downloads from the Internet. This portfolio is also proof since it was also done on the computer. I've also included a disk of clip art, the grading program, and the word search program I'm currently considering using in my classroom.

Variety Is Vital

Document representation should include a variety of carefully selected items of teacher and student work illustrating key indicators. Each artifact must be accompanied by captions and written reflections that explain the contents. Including a teacher-made test without explanation is not enough. Within a subdivision on assessment, the developer should provide diverse supporting captions/reflections including information about the ability to (a) develop an assessment philosophy, (b) compose a test that meets state/district guidelines for the curriculum area, (c) design a grading scale, (d) analyze the scores, (e) demonstrate how individual differences were met, and finally, (f) reflect through a self-analysis of the entire process.

The portfolio allows the reader to understand the complex thinking behind the teaching process. By linking theory and application, documentation of sound instruction is enhanced, providing the plan for professional reflection and growth. Self-analysis is crucial because evaluation of teachers is frequently a yearly "duty," generally designed for promotion or nonrenewal, rather than teacher improvement. Knowing why a particular lesson was effective or ineffective is essential for continued success and further improvement.

Typical Items to Include

Although each organization has individual guidelines for portfolio development, some commonalties can be found. The following are typical items required during the portfolio development process:

1. Introductory letter
2. Table of contents
3. Résumé

4. Transcript

5. Formal evaluations
   a. Clinical teaching experiences
   b. Student teaching
   c. Self-evaluation/reflection
   d. Supervising teacher
   e. Administrator (if experienced teacher)

6. Philosophies
   a. Teaching
   b. Discipline/classroom management
   c. Parent involvement
   d. Assessment
   e. Multicultural

7. Letters of recommendation

8. Competencies or standards

9. Videotape of teaching

10. Personal accomplishments/autobiography

11. Student work samples

Though various categories may be required, the selection of which artifacts best supports the individual category is left to the student's discretion. Early in the teaching program, students should begin collecting all artifacts that are indicative of educational growth.

The difference between a portfolio and résumé is that the portfolio provides the "proof" that these skills or experiences exist. Essential to portfolio development is documentation. If a preservice teacher's philosophy states that all children can learn, then the portfolio should provide the proof that the individual acted on that belief. That proof could be demonstrated through lesson plans, adaptations made for individual students, notes from students and parents, IEPs, teaching evaluations, personal reflections, or even a videotaped teaching segment. Show me. Prove it. That process makes a portfolio different from other evaluations.

Voluntary Items

A second question to ask when planning a portfolio is, "What items do I *want* to include?" These would include additional artifacts that present information about individual qualifications or experiences that do not fit into other required categories. A word of warning: Be selective! Including too much information can be as damaging as including too little. Busy people will be reviewing the documents, so include only those artifacts showcasing skills as they relate to the original purpose.

Sometimes optional items are listed as additional information or personal accomplishments. When answering a job vacancy notice, adapt the portfolio and cover letter to align with the skills or credentials listed in the section, "minimum qualifications," and if possible, "preferred." Tailoring the portfolio and résumé to meet individual employer advertisements increases the likelihood of getting an interview.

For example, if the job application is for an assistant football coach, and you have spent the last 4 years working as a volunteer student coach at a junior high school, that is a fact that would be pertinent to the job description. If the application does not include a place for volunteer or community service, adding your experience in the résumé or portfolio may provide a needed advantage, especially if all applicants are equal in regard to years of experience. An endorsement letter from the coach would also be something to include, as it validates expertise, interpersonal skills, and personal qualities. A team photograph or local news article including your name would also record that experience.

Documenting educational experiences is vital to portfolio development. Without documentation and reflection, the final result will only be a scrapbook or a glorified résumé. Thinking seriously about past experiences and how those relate to the educational setting is necessary (see Chapter 6). These past experiences shape philosophies, behaviors, and attitudes. They also provide preservice and novice teachers with a wealth of real teaching skills when viewed with a professional eye.

Other Possible Contents of a Teaching Portfolio

Remember that the portfolio is not just a collection, but rather a selection. The items typically chosen for inclusion in this category are to showcase skills. Unless the teaching portfolio is purely developmental in nature, it contains snippets to represent the very best of each category.

The portfolio may be thought of as a tool to assist in blending theories and practices of teaching and learning. No rigid rules or guidelines exist as to what or how much to include in a portfolio. The primary objective is first to collect and then to select, including only those things that reflect competencies or individual goals. One must, however, be cautious when using classroom-produced artifacts to protect the confidentiality and privacy of individual students.

The portfolio will provide a representation of growth as an educator and establish a foundation for goal setting, reflection, and introspection. The portfolio may provide the basis for determining the student's progress in, and completion of, the program. The following list is not intended to be inclusive, and the final determination of what to include lies with the individual portfolio developer. (Although most items could be used by a beginning or an experienced teacher, items indicated with an asterisk (*) are primarily for experienced teachers.)

Artifacts From Oneself

1. Cover letter: a written statement describing the contents of the portfolio and how the contents demonstrate the achievement of the goals.

2. Philosophies: statement of beliefs including, but not limited to, philosophy of teaching, philosophy of parent involvement, multicultural statement, philosophy of reading, philosophy of discipline, and philosophy of the use of technology.

3. Transcripts: one from each college or university attended.

4. Résumé: objective, educational background (certification test results, if passed; state license, if granted), *work/teaching experience (tutoring, student teaching, grade levels, hours of public school activities/observations, professional workshops attended or hours, volunteer activities involving children), organizations, honors, references (designate relation of each listed such as supervising teacher, *principal, university advisor).

5. Goals: program, professional, and personal (both long- and short-term). Include plans for continued professional development.

6. Self-Assessments/reflections: narratives that demonstrate self-analysis of teaching techniques and steps taken to improve.

7. Videotape or audiotape of teaching segment with reflective narrative.

8. Copies of teaching materials: include different types of teaching materials and evaluative instruments developed.

9. Lesson plans: highlight with captions a particular area included, such as provisions for cooperative learning, higher-order thinking activities, provisions for individual differences, linkage to state learner outcomes, and so forth.

10. Case studies: *in-depth individual study, tutoring experiences.

11. Photographs: interactive bulletin boards; student projects; learning centers; informal classroom shots; action photos; artistic models or paintings; things that demonstrate interaction with students, faculty, or community.

12. Professional development: list of workshops and conferences attended, *special areas of expertise or training, subscriptions to professional journals and organizations, self-initiated visits/volunteerism, and substitute teaching experiences.

13. Record of innovative methods: new strategies or programs implemented, such as team teaching, cross-curriculum activities, peer tutoring program, and so forth.

14. Record-keeping artifacts: rubrics, checklists, grade book excerpts, anything that documents ability to manage or assess students' progress.

15. Assessment examples: various types of tests: objective, multiple choice, true/false, matching, essay; rubrics; contracts; participation;

and various forms of alternative assessment used to evaluate student progress.

16. Parent communication materials: sample parent newsletters, report cards/progress reports/notes sent home with individual students, parent-teacher conference schedules, parent volunteer activities initiated.

17. Professional writing: anything published.

18. Educational travel: appropriate if travel correlates with teaching assignment.

19. Technology activities: samples or disks including electronic grade book, grade-analysis sheet, templates for lesson plans, copies of favorite Web sites including student's sites to be used for instruction, printouts of Internet research or Web pages developed, a lesson that shows how computers/Internet will be used to enhance instruction.

20. Evidence of commitment to diversity: description of multicultural experiences including information relative to experiences with languages other than English, travel, volunteer experience, or work experience with other cultures.

21. *Statement of teaching responsibilities: list of courses taught including syllabi, as well as recent evidence of classroom activities and personal teaching style.

22. Description of current scholarship: documented artifacts such as self-reflective narratives; *list of presentations at scholarly meetings; awards and recognition; *funded grant proposals; other evidence of contributions to students, programs, and other professionals.

Artifacts From Others

1. Formal evaluations: *evidence from administrators, supervising teachers, peers, and students evaluating teaching and assessment, human relations, professionalism, and classroom management.

2. Informal critiques: samples of assignments with written comments from instructors or peers.

3. Solicited and unsolicited endorsements: letters of recommendation, letters/notes from students, peers, supervisors, and faculty that document demonstrated commitment to high educational or personal standards.

4. Media: newspaper or magazine articles that validate activities and professional and personal self-development.

5. Honors: scholarship or grant recipient, teaching awards, leadership roles in professional organizations, community service awards, or nominations for exceptional achievement.

6. Additional credentials: *certified trainer for various educational programs.

Products of Excellent Teaching

(A word of caution: When including student work in the portfolio, keep in mind the Family Educational and Privacy Act (FERPA) of 1974 guidelines for confidentiality. If you share the portfolio with others, then confidentiality of any written materials should be maintained. Student names should be eliminated when using personal samples.)

1. Pre/post student scores demonstrating improvement.
2. Record of students who demonstrate success in later endeavors.
3. Letters that justify the importance of one's influence.
4. Committee or task force assignments because of instructional innovation.
5. Positive comparative analysis of before and after student attitudes toward learning.
6. Invitations to present in area of expertise.
7. Student work that demonstrates a high degree of understanding of the scientific process or concepts, analysis/awareness of social studies, and integrates mathematical or technological concepts.

Contributions to Personal and Professional Growth

Geltner (1993) wrote in her paper, "Integrating Formative Portfolio Assessment, Reflective Practice and Cognitive Coaching into Preservice Preparation,"

> The experience of documenting one's own activities and considering their meaning as part of one's total growth places responsibility where it most properly lies—with the learner. Further, portfolio assessment permits inclusion of experiences ranging far beyond those possible within the space and time confines of the classroom.

The portfolio is an opportunity to gather evidence of developing teaching skills and to reflect on personal growth. As the time approaches for the culminating portfolio presentation, the collection of documents, reflective papers, and artifacts should confirm for the presenter and others a comprehensive and sophisticated understanding of the teaching process.

Planning

Documenting professional growth in a portfolio format requires special methods for collecting various artifacts. The cardinal rule is to keep *every-*

thing. As administrators are frequently reminded, "If it isn't documented, it didn't happen." The priority then is first collect, then select. Accumulating "evidence" is the beginning of the professional portfolio.

Collection

Many students choose to keep assignments, articles, critiques, time logs, evaluations, and photos all together in one central location, most usually a cardboard box, and frequently under the bed or in the car trunk. Because of time constraints, the material is saved, albeit in a haphazard fashion, for future use.

Other students keep materials together in notebooks with pocket fillers holding bulkier items such as video/audiotapes, games, and teaching units. The notebooks are labeled with the course name, and students associate the contents of the notebook with the course requirements.

Type A students file each project in alphabetical order in a filing cabinet or accordion file folder. Some who really understand how the portfolio is put together organize their collection based on the teacher education program competencies. For example, items that provide documentation for professional growth are filed under the professionalism competency. Here, one would find past conference booklets, flyers of speeches attended, newspaper articles about the conferences, professional development attendance verification, and the like. Invitations and cards representing membership in scholarly organizations also would be found. Service in education-related clubs also would be documented. Any photos taken at these events also would be included with the name of the event and the date on the back.

During the collection phase, portfolio materials can be stored using any method that suits the developer. The goal, however, is retrieval when needed. Some students prefer thumbing through everything before finding the artifact they need, whereas others prefer to narrow down and categorize their "stuff" prior to the search for the right document.

The process of portfolio development is organic. It changes daily with the individual developer's needs and interests. A goal of all development, however, is to assist students and faculty in submitting appropriate and relevant materials.

Selection

Assisting students and teachers in selecting appropriate artifacts is an important part of the portfolio process. When the portfolio is based on specific standards that highlight and demonstrate teaching skills, a portfolio planner can be used (see Resource D).

The planner is used to aid developers in (a) describing the evidence to be submitted for each competency, (b) demonstrating how the evidence reflects their learning, and (c) validating how that knowledge impacted their behavior.

Planners are used collaboratively during individual and small group conferences with peers and faculty advisers. They serve as a written focus or a plan for fine-tuning selected artifacts to determine their appropriateness, and also as a benchmark with required signatures and dates to prevent last-minute cramming. Often, the professional exchanges between students and faculty assist students in examining their contributions in a scholarly and insightful manner. Requiring documentation of both theory and application to link with the artifacts is often overwhelming, so the collaborative efforts and support of all involved parties are of great benefit.

Many students have reported difficulties in making connections between required activities, theory, and practice, then applying them to specified criteria such as the required program competencies. The higher-order thinking process demands analyzing, synthesizing, comparing, categorizing, and creating to demonstrate a thoughtful, deliberate attempt to present the "thinking" side of learning. Although few educators would debate its importance, this process is still not frequently embedded in our student evaluations. Perhaps the infrequency of such rigorous assessment is why students experience such difficulty.

The following is the result of one student's journey toward completion of her first step in formally documenting a required program competency at East Central University, Ada, Oklahoma. Jama Hutchins' (1997) Instructional Competency I Portfolio Sample includes the integration of artifacts, theory, and application.

Competency 12

The teacher understands the process of continuous lifelong learning, the concept of making learning enjoyable, and the need for a willingness to change when the change leads to greater student learning development.

Artifact for Competency 12

"The following photographs represent a learning center designed for my Methods of Elementary Science class. I presented it to Mrs. Deborah Berry's third-grade students at Hanna Elementary on April 28, 1997. I included it as an artifact for Competency 12 because I feel it supports the concept of making learning enjoyable and shows the need for a willingness to change when the change leads to greater student learning and development."

Theory for Competency 12

"The use of centers in the classroom is an excellent way to gauge the effectiveness of learning. Successful learning comes from doing, and centers can provide this opportunity. Centers may be used as a self-selected activity, a follow-up to a teacher's lesson, an activity in place of a regular assignment, or as an enrichment activity. Centers also encourage children to make decisions and to think independently. These types of activities are welcome changes in most classrooms, and children enjoy them immensely. Using centers enables a teacher to identify easily any problems with subject matter or content. Children have different learning styles and strengths, and the better suited your lessons are to those varying styles, the better your students will be able to learn. Centers allow for modifications to be made when necessary and are relatively easily to implement. Students take an active role in their learning in these types of activities and welcome the opportunity to experience something new and exciting.

"In researching this subject, the consensus seems to favor the use of centers. In the textbook *Early Childhood Education*, the author states, 'Children from infancy through age eight to ten can benefit from clearly delineated, organized, thematic areas called learning centers.' It went on to detail some of the many advantages of using these activities. Some included creating a cooperative atmosphere for the classroom and providing numerous opportunities for the teacher to observe the students in action. This enables assessment and evaluation of activities as well as student progress. Learning centers inside the classroom provide students with a venue to engage in activities that support learning. They foster an atmosphere of camaraderie encouraging students to turn to one another to solve problems. Again, they allow students to take charge of their own materials and work, while providing teachers opportunities to observe students and plan individual or group instruction."

Application for Competency 12

"The use of centers in modern classrooms can be an effective teaching tool. I have seen successful centers in use and have presented my own in classrooms. Centers are enjoyable to students on many levels. They provide a variety of learning experiences and materials, encouraging children to explore, experiment, discover, and socialize in their individual ways. As they do so, teachers can observe differences in learning styles as well as children's responses to various activities. This enables them to adapt or change activities, as is necessary.

"I chose to use my own learning center for application of Competency 12. I feel it demonstrates the need for learning to be enjoyable and illustrates the need for change when that change leads to greater student understanding. The students at Hanna Elementary greatly enjoyed the center I brought to their school and asked if I would make them another one before I finished my Field I observations. My cooperating teacher and I did create a plant center before I left, and the students were very pleased with our efforts. The aspect of enjoyment could be seen in the faces of the children and heard in the excitement of their voices. It was rewarding to see the students actively participating in the activities and sharing their findings with one another. They surprised me with the amount of information they compiled on the human body topic. They took the activities seriously and worked diligently on each assignment they chose. This experience was very beneficial to me and enabled me to see firsthand the advantages in using centers.

"The center also enabled me to make modifications, as they became necessary, to ensure greater understanding for the students. One of the original activities I chose for the center was labeling skeletal systems. It was evident immediately that the activity was too detailed and time consuming. Instead of the tedious labeling activity, I modified the center and had the children construct their own bone models with basic materials. This was much more satisfactory, and the children did an outstanding job on the task. Another problem I ran into was the use of research materials for some of the students. A few of them had great difficulty researching their chosen topics based on their reading levels. This called for Plan B. Again, the activity was modified to accommodate the needs of these students. The teacher and I provided additional resources that the children were better able to understand. Overall, the center was a success. The students and I came away a little more knowledgeable about the subject and what it takes to make a learning center work for everyone. I feel this experience was invaluable and stressed not only the importance for enjoyable learning, but also the need for change when it leads to greater understanding."

This student's narrative reflects authentic reflections about her experiences as she related how she applied the theory of the university classroom to the practical experience of the elementary classroom. Her captioned artifacts also focused on Competency 12 with all components evident.

Portfolio Length

The debate about the appropriate length of a teaching portfolio continues. Some contend that because a portfolio evolves over a period of time, it should be quite lengthy and inclusive enough to show growth (20 or more pages). Others argue that for undergraduates, a portfolio will be primarily used to secure employment and should be concise (10 or fewer pages). Their argument is that principals and human relations officers have neither the time, space, nor inclination to peruse a notebook full of information, tapes, disks, and so forth. Even those who will be using the portfolio to substantiate program competencies have varying opinions about the proper length of a student portfolio.

Findings reveal that the majority of institutions stipulate categories, require inclusion of specified documents and artifacts, and often even outline the exact format to be used, but rarely mandate minimum or maximum page requirements. Because the portfolio is a professional endeavor, much flexibility is afforded during the compilation of materials. The how-many-words-per-page mind-set is not for portfolio developers.

Levels of Portfolio Development

The portfolio should be thorough enough to cover the topic, but concise and businesslike in the approach and presentation of materials. One way to determine how long a portfolio should be is again to consider the intended use of the portfolio.

Level I Portfolio: Initial Employment Visit

A Level I portfolio would be used primarily for employment purposes. This portfolio would be given to an administrator at the time an applicant applies for a teaching position. It would include the basic information needed for initial employment consideration. The contents would include items such as a cover letter, transcript, résumé, and some writing samples of one's philosophy of education or philosophy of classroom management.

Level II Portfolio: Interview

A Level II portfolio would be used when an applicant is considered as a finalist for a teaching position. This portfolio would be an expanded version of Level I, personalized for the individual district, as well as a vehicle to be used during an interview or for showcasing existing skills and past achievements or experience.

Administrative Views

The March 5, 1997, *Education Week on the Web* article, "Portfolios Playing Increasing Role In Teacher Hiring," by Linda Jacobson, reports that of the more than 1,000 personnel administrators and superintendents polled, few required portfolios from applicants. However, researchers from the University of Iowa have found that portfolios are becoming an "important ingredient" in the teacher-hiring process.

More than half of the administrative respondents indicated that they are more likely to request or accept a portfolio once the applicant had become a finalist for a position. Some of the most useful items, according to the respondents, were student work, classroom photographs, statements about teaching style, philosophy, and personal goals. Caution was advised about overloading portfolios. Information contained should be "minimal and meaningful."

A misconception exists about how much a portfolio should contain. One should not have to bring in boxes and boxes of materials to validate skills. For brevity's sake, after an individual concept has been documented, additional materials can be recorded in an appendix with links to additional materials.

When deciding to create a professional portfolio, using the provided checklist can assist the student in deciding on the purpose, the standards that will be used, collection and selection, and the length of the final product.

Personal Portfolio Checklist

- What is the purpose of my portfolio?
- What required items do I have to include?
- What optional items do I want to include?
- What artifacts do I already have that will support my portfolio?
- Do I need to collect additional samples or participate in other activities in order to complete the goals/competencies of the portfolio?
- Have I developed a plan for collecting artifacts?
- How will I organize my portfolio?
- How will I select representative artifacts?
- What are the length stipulations for the portfolio?
- What type of materials should I collect?

6

Self-Assessment of the Artifacts and Design

Jenny worked hard trying to collect as many different materials as possible for her portfolio. She had gathered photos of herself working with children, samples of units that she had taught, and critiques from her public school and university supervisors. In fact, the boxes were beginning to take over her dorm room. She never imagined that one could collect so much stuff from 2 years of college classes, clinical experiences, and personal accomplishments.

Although each student had been given a list of program competencies and was told to document each one with two samples of their best work, Jenny was having difficulty correlating materials with competencies. It seemed that she could use some items in more than one category, whereas other documents appeared to be useless.

She had learned a great deal through some non-school-related activities, but they did not seem to fit into any particular category. She wondered how professors were going to evaluate the portfolios when each student had so many different experiences.

Were the experiences she had satisfactory? Would she include the "right" documents to support her learning? How could she know if her reflections were on target? She was becoming very frustrated and uneasy about this big project.

Reflections of Who You Are

Once portfolio materials have been collected, the real work begins. One must determine how all of these artifacts can be assembled into a shining profile of you: who you are, what you have experienced, and how you feel about teaching. Because the documents will ultimately endorse an individual's teaching, application, and organization skills, materials must be deliberately and thoughtfully selected.

Many events have shaped your thinking about education, so the manner in which you choose to present them frequently determines the success of the portfolio. The process begins with the obvious physical considerations and ends with the final assessment. Does this portfolio reveal the scope of my learning, both formal and informal? Your professional reflection is mirrored from the type of paper and design elements chosen to the writing style and selected artifacts. The organization of your portfolio also is a revelation. Your portfolio will most definitely send a message to the reader. The goal is to ensure it is a message indicative of your past, present, and future.

Accentuate the Positive

Students frequently feel inadequate when trying to validate specific required competencies. Because student education experiences are often limited, with minimal classroom time accumulated, some mistakenly assume validation of such goals, such as the Oklahoma General Competencies for Teacher Licensure and Certification (Oklahoma State Board of Education, 1996; see Resource B), are impossible.

Students comment, "How can I show that I understand curriculum integration when I have only taught one unit?" or "How can I prove that I understand the importance of fostering positive interaction with school colleagues, parents/families, and organizations in the community when I have limited contact with them?" One way to assist students in recognizing their current level of expertise is by conducting workshops, seminars, courses, and conferences where a positive exchange of information and concerns can be communicated. Sharing samples of acceptable levels of work as well as some that are exemplary or below expected levels provides a construct from which students can begin to understand the portfolio process.

However limited, students often have learned a variety of skills that until now were not considered as "teaching" attributes. Small groups and individualized portfolio planning conferences such as portfolio peer groups (see Chapter 4) have proven to be instrumental in aiding students as they prepare their portfolios.

Guided Professional Conversations

A necessary component of portfolio development is the professional conversations of the student with peers, professors, practicing teachers, and mentors. Although students have diverse experiences, the competencies or program goals are standard. Therefore, each student must assess which experiences will reveal growth or expertise in a particular area. No one can fully know another's past or how that past affected his or her attitude and learning. This step is a solitary examination that requires reflection and thought, as discussed in Chapter 4.

Integrating Nonteaching Experiences

Underestimating the strength of non-education-related experiences was demonstrated when a student was required to validate an understanding of Competency 13, which deals with the legal aspects of teaching; rights of students and parents/families; and the legal rights and responsibilities of the teacher. She was very frustrated because, according to her, she had virtually no experience in dealing with any legal issues related to education.

Using the portfolio planner (see Resource D) as a conversation focus, the student was asked to relate any legal issues that dealt with rights or responsibilities. The student, Cristy Gilreath (1997), then recalled that during her time as an Upward Bound counselor, her job description actually included many legal responsibilities of a teacher. The following excerpt was written after an individual conference with her instructor.

> Our orientation consisted of a lot of rule reading and instruction on how to fill out the mountain of forms they gave us. There were forms for everything. Then we were made aware of the legal aspects. These forms were for the protection of us as people with privileged information as well as the students and their families.
>
> We had to sign confidentiality agreements. This was to make sure the students' social security numbers and other personal information were safe. We also had to document all time spent alone with students. For our safety, the director suggested that we keep a contact diary.

She's Got It! She's Really Got It!

The student continued by linking her Foundations of Education class knowledge, specifically the Family Educational Rights and Privacy Act of 1974 (Family Compliance Office, 1974), with her previous experiences as a summer counselor in order to validate her learning. "Before learning about FERPA, I thought that just about anyone could look at your grades. I feel now that I can better understand some of the legal aspects of teaching, including the rights of students and their parents/families when seeking information from educational records."

Document Peripheral Experiences

After one or two portfolio conferences, most students begin to understand how their past has influenced their learning. Some examples of student learning experiences that have valuable "carryover" include the following:

- Substitute teaching (any grades)
- Church-related teaching (any age or specialty such as choir)

- Civic-related experiences (Boys/Girls Clubs, YMCA, Big Brother/Sister, Boy/Girl Scouts, mentoring)
- Volunteer work (grades Pre-K through 12; hospital or community events)
- Counseling (summer camps)
- Tutoring (any age)
- Leadership roles in social clubs (any appropriate, with special emphasis on education related fraternities)
- Committee work (include role and responsibility)
- Supervisory roles (work related or volunteer)
- Presentation skills (speeches, panel participant, presenter)
- Clinical teaching
- Student teaching
- Job experiences (specific skills, especially technology, training, or human relations)

At times, students need assistance in processing and sifting through the enormous amount of possible information. Directed conferences held with peers and teachers greatly enhance the student's ability to relate previous learning to required objectives. The hardest parts of the process are the student's leap from the theory to the application and verifying their understanding of how one complements the other.

Determination of Purpose and Audience

When compiling information for the portfolio, think about the purpose of the portfolio as well as the person or persons who will be evaluating the materials (see Chapter 3). The chosen documents should reflect the expected outcome.

- If the portfolio is to be used for employment purposes, consider which artifacts will enhance your job skills. Will they convince a principal to hire you?
- If it is for reflection, consider which documents support your self-assessment and growth. Will they prove to a professor that you have substantially thought about your performance and developed a plan of improvement, then demonstrated and documented that growth in the requested areas?
- If the portfolio is for program evaluation, consider which materials verify your expertise of basic competencies. Will they justify a peer/faculty committee in granting you certification or graduation to the next level?
- If it is for evaluation purposes only, consider which items meet specified grading criteria. Will they provide a teacher/evaluator with adequate information that you have met course objectives?

- If the portfolio is for tenure purposes, consider which expected categories are to be included. Will they convince a review board that you have fully and expertly fulfilled promotion/tenure requirements?

Possible Portfolio Evaluators

Many organizations require various combinations of groups and individuals to evaluate portfolios. Some include only individual professors, whereas others mandate a team of portfolio evaluators. Some use only internal evaluators whereas others hire outside consultants. Many institutions incorporate both individual and group evaluations. Common education teachers and administrators, as well as your peers, may be members of an evaluation panel. When applying for a teaching job, the school principal may be the one who assesses the portfolio. There are no specific rules for determining who evaluates except each organization's own policies. An exception is where state or national mandates require, through legislation, the evaluators and the criteria for judging the portfolios.

One has no control over who evaluates, but one most certainly does have the option of asking questions about the "who" and the "how" of the portfolio evaluation. Including documents that are important to that individual/team evaluator(s) are vital to the success of the portfolio.

Possible Evaluation Instruments

The number of instruments used to evaluate portfolios is as numerous as the organizations requiring them. Many types of assessment instruments are used—developed by individual school districts or departments, teacher-made, and designed as mandated outgrowths from state or national committees. Some include checklists, rubrics, Likert-type scales, oral and written narratives, formal evaluation forms, and informal feedback. Others assign a point value, percentage, or letter grade to each criterion based on how fully the topic is covered, and still others have a pass/fail format.

Critics of portfolio assessment argue that its subjectivity and the lack of standardization make it difficult to compare one portfolio with another. However, those concerns are somewhat alleviated by requiring specific documents. Yet, there remains a problem in how to make portfolio evaluation as reliable and valid as possible, given their individualistic contents.

A solution, according to Doolittle (1994), is to use Likert-type evaluation forms based on the mandated items. Then, the categorized items are weighted and ratings are combined to provide an overall score, allowing a more objective method of comparison.

Informing oneself about the evaluation process is comparable to looking at a map before taking a journey. Know what is expected and, within the expectation, the various levels that are acceptable. In planning your portfolio, familiarize yourself with the intended outcomes. Determine what it will look like physically, what format it will have, what required categories and mandatory artifacts will be included, and what guidelines will be used for organization, and then personalize.

Sample Evaluation Instruments

The rubric seems to provide students with necessary information about the levels of portfolio assessment (see Resource F). Providing and sharing samples of each level of development will assist students in gaining insight as to what is exemplary or marginal. As students practice evaluating the various documents of their peers, a clear picture emerges regarding the level of expertise of each portfolio document. The following sample rubric with assigned point values was used for evaluating a reflection and observation of student field activities.

Standards for Evaluating Field Activities
Observation and Reflection Reports Level III

18-20 points:	Report is indicative of exceptional insight communicated in a creative and accurate manner, applying previously learned information. Product is professionally presented. Documentation is exact and thorough.
15-17 points:	Report fulfills all basic requirements with good written communication skills and is easy to follow. Shows evidence of some reflection of effective practices. Accurately interprets information. Product is neatly presented. Documentation supports reports.
14-12 points:	Report does not meet two or more of the requested items. Writing includes some inappropriate or insignificant comments. Not enough information gathered for an accurate assessment. Contains little or no reflection. Product is somewhat messy. Documentation is evident, but not thorough.
8-11 points:	Report fails to address three or more of required items. Information gathered is too brief. Contains little or no application of knowledge of previous appropriate practices. Reflections are inaccurate or shallow. Writing is difficult to follow and not carefully written. Documentation fails to support findings or is too sketchy to validate results.
Below 8 points:	Report is missing or lacking in essential items necessary for evaluation. Glaring inconsistencies exist between data and summary. Report is not clearly organized but moves reader randomly with little or no thought to expected outcome. No reflection is apparent. Product appears to be "thrown together" with little or no pride. Documentation is sparse or nonexistent.

Another instrument was used as the first checkpoint for a cohort of beginning teacher education students. It is a combination of a checklist, formal evaluation criteria, Likert-type scale, and rubric. The document also contains a compilation of general information such as a transcript, grade point average, and field-hour documentation.

The first level of evaluation is standardized with mandated items and with little or no opportunity for students to individualize. The second and third levels of portfolio evaluation progressively lead students to self-selection of items based on specific teacher education competencies, as well as some required guidelines and artifacts.

TEAMS Evaluation Criteria

I. Résumé

    Organization: ___ Outstanding   ___ Fair   ___ Below average

    Basic information: ___ Outstanding   ___ Fair   ___ Below average

    Neatness: ___ Outstanding   ___ Fair   ___ Below average

II. Current Transcript

    GPA:

    Total number of hours:

III. Statement of Beliefs

    ___ Well-organized and appropriate with high degree of understanding correlated to teaching

    ___ Adequately developed philosophy, congruent with present level of preservice training

    ___ Inappropriate: fails to adequately demonstrate understanding of educational processes

IV. Recommentations

    ___ Outstanding

    ___ Average

    ___ Below Average

V. Response Statement

    ___ Well-organized with appropriate references demonstrating a high degree of personal insight, easy to follow

    ___ Adequately developed philosophy with basic information presented

    ___ Inappropriate; fails to communicate pertinent information

VI. Goals

___ Well-developed, precise, sequential, and visionary

___ Accurate, essential steps included yet lacks personalization

___ Thought process not evident, lacks depth

VII. Evaluation from Mentor (taken from formal evaluation sheet, 4 = highest level)

Punctuality	1	2	3	4
Appearance	1	2	3	4
Cooperation	1	2	3	4
Professionalism	1	2	3	4
Initiative	1	2	3	4
Attendance	1	2	3	4

Strengths:

Concerns:

Recommendation:

VIII. Documentation of Field Hours

___ Exceeded required hours

___ Met required hours

___ Failed to meet required hours

IX. Writing Mechanics (grammar, capitalization, punctuation, spelling)

___ No glaring errors exist; grammar, usage, and spelling are generally correct; punctuation is smooth. Easy to read with good flow of language.

___ Reasonable control over a limited range of conventions. Grammar and usage problems are not sufficiently serious to distort meaning; spelling is usually correct. Terminal punctuation is usually correct; internal punctuation is inconsistent.

___ Errors make reading difficult. Errors in grammar, usage, spelling, and punctuation affect meaning.

X. Ideas and Content Development

___ Product is clear and focused with (1) shared insights and important details, (2) writer in control of topic, and (3) ideas shaped and connected.

___ Product is clear and focused even though development is limited. Ideas are reasonably clear but not detailed, personalized, or expanded. Main points lack originality and more information is needed to "fill in the blanks."

___ Product has no clear purpose with repetition and limited information. Everything is equally important. The topic is not defined in a meaningful way.

XI. Organization

____ Product order and structure are very easy to follow with information delivered at just the right moment.

____ Product order and structure moves reader without undue confusion. The introduction and conclusion are there but are weak. Pacing is fairly well controlled although too much time is devoted to the obvious. Connection between ideas is somewhat fuzzy, but organization does not get in the way of main points.

____ Product lacks a clear sense of direction and is hard to follow. No organization. There is no introduction or conclusion, and there are confusing connections between ideas. Great deal of time devoted to minor details, making it difficult to understand the main point.

Students were given oral and written feedback about their portfolio at this particular level. If deficient in a particular category, students were required (with the assistance of an advisor), to develop a plan of improvement. Because all written documents were kept on disk, students were asked to correct any composition errors so the documents could be error-free and used for later portfolio development.

Some students recognized the need to develop their composition skills and began attending tutorial sessions in the campus writing lab, whereas others saw the need for a change in attitude or developed a time management system to make better use of time.

The initial evaluation also provided an opportunity for individual students to self-evaluate and determine if they were satisfied with their professional growth. One-on-one, students were, for the most part, brutally honest about their own abilities, and many even chose to drop out of the program because they recognized that teaching was much more demanding and intense than they originally thought. Others seemed inspired by the challenge and went beyond original expectations.

Respecting the integrity of individual student choices while guiding them to examine their own levels of development provided an intimate look at student aspirations. Many personal characteristics, not evident in other areas of classroom evaluation, were examined, dissected, and revealed. The introspection and resulting plans for individual personal growth were evident.

The next checklist demonstrates specified items required for another group of students in their first level of portfolio development. Each student in the teacher education program had to include the items in order to pass the course. If a category was not included, students were given an incomplete grade until Level I of the portfolio development was complete. The required competencies were the General Competencies for Teacher Licensure and Certification (Oklahoma State Board of Education, 1996; see Resource B).

Portfolio Contents Checklist for Instructional Competency I

The following items must be included, or the portfolio will be returned and an incomplete will be given until all items are included. A check mark indicates that the item was included.

___ Portfolio notebook

___ Table of contents

___ Divider pages with tabs

___ Résumé

___ Current transcript

___ List of general program competencies for teacher education

___ Documented Competency 12
      2 artifacts
      2 theories or rationales (student theory and expert theory)
      2 applications with personal reflections

___ Documented Competency 13
      2 artifacts
      2 theories or rationales (student theory and expert theory)
      2 applications with personal reflections

___ Short- and long-term goals

___ Preprofessional Field Experience Evaluation Forms I, II, III

___ Preprofessional Field Experience Record Form (time sheet)

In addition, the student was required to present the Level I portfolio to a team of evaluators including two professors and a peer. The instrument used to evaluate the oral presentation of the portfolio for beginning teachers is as follows:

Portfolio Oral Presentation Evaluation, Level I

Use the following scale to evaluate the presentation:

2 – The presenter did this very well.
1 – The presenter did this.
0 – The presenter did not do this.

The presenter:

___ 1. Clearly summarized his or her experiences in the program.

___ 2. Clearly indicated important things he or she learned in the program.

___ 3. Clearly indicated areas to work on for continued professional development.

___ 4. Clearly demonstrated thoughtful reflection about experiences in the program.

___ 5. Clearly indicated an understanding of what an exemplary teacher does.

___ 6. Was well organized.

___ 7. Spoke well, using language relatively free from obvious errors in grammar, word choice, and pronunciation.

___ Total points

I consider this portfolio presentation: ___ Satisfactory   ___ Unsatisfactory

Evaluator's Signature _____

Evaluator's Status   ___ Peer   ___ Faculty:

_____

(Each student was also rated on the level of documented evidence of the competencies. These were presented both in writing and orally during the presentation.)

The levels of expertise should be evaluated by the following:

Distinguished/exemplary (4): The teacher proved exceptional competence through the inclusion of pertinent information and critical assessment of documentation.

Proficient (3): The teacher included important evidence and documentation to support an above-average understanding of the competency.

Essential/basic (2): The teacher included cursory documentation with minimal understanding.

Unsatisfactory (1): The teacher failed to demonstrate a basic understanding of the competency.

Additional comments and recommendations:

The next sample was used as an exit evaluation just prior to graduation. The evaluation team consisted of two public school teachers, one university professor, and a student peer. Students were assigned 30-minute time slots to share the portfolio and respond to any questions from the committee. Students were required to dress professionally, as they would during a teacher interview. After the presentations, students were given written feedback about the strengths and weaknesses of the portfolio and presentation. Personal conferences were also arranged for those who requested them.

TEAMS Portfolio Evaluation—Student, Level 4

Check or circle selected level or expertise.

I.   Cover Page/Notebook Appearance
     Exceptional   Average   Below average

II. Cover letter/introductory
     ___ Exceptional/interesting/appealing
     ___ Average information/no errors but no pizzazz
     ___ Below average/too little information/some errors

III. Table of Contents
     ___ Accurate/neat/well organized
     ___ Basic/some needed information left out
     ___ Below average or nonexistent

IV. Résumé
     ___ Exceptional: outstanding information and organization
     ___ Average: includes basics but not well organized
     ___ Below average: lacks essential information or contains errors

V.   Transcript
     ___ Included
     ___ Not included

VI. Critiques
     Teacher evaluation of student teaching (This information was taken from mentor teacher evaluation and categories based on the Residency Year Teacher Evaluation Instrument.)

     Teaching and
     assessment: ___ Exceptional ___ Average ___ Below average
     Public relations: ___ Exceptional ___ Average ___ Below average

Professionalism: ___ Exceptional ___ Average ___ Below average

Classroom management: ___ Exceptional ___ Average ___ Below average

Strengths:

Concerns:

Student reflection of student teaching

___ Sophisticated understanding

___ Adequate understanding but superficial

___ Misunderstanding of key ideas

VII. Philosophy

___ Well organized and appropriate with high degree of understanding

___ Adequately developed philosophy but does not reflect an experienced view

___ Weakly constructed; lacks depth

VIII. Letters of Recommendation

___ Peer ___ Public School Teacher ___ University Professor

Key characteristics mentioned:

IX. Competencies

Student-selected (minimum number required must be met):

School Structure Curriculum Growth and Development

Exceptionalities Diversity Instruction Learning

Media and Technology Assessment Classroom Management

Professionalism

Best Evidence (list student's specific entries and support for mastery of that competency)

___ Student shows substantial evidence of critically assessing and selecting pertinent documents and reflections reveal an insightful and thoughtful educator.

___ Student shows some evidence of selecting important documents to support their competence in the selected areas.

___ Student fails to substantiate an understanding, reflection, and documentation of the competencies.

X. Personal Accomplishments

___ Items reflect a representation of the student not seen in other artifacts, including shared insights, important details, and a revelation of student thoughts.

___ Items are limited and lacking in personalization. Reflection lacks depth

___ Items appear to be randomly selected without a plan or an explanation of the importance of their inclusion.

XI. Anecdote—Closing

___ Exceptional

___ Average

___ Below average

Comments:

XII. Overall Review of the Portfolio

If you were interviewing this person for a teaching position, what comments would you make regarding the oral presentation and/or portfolio documents presented by this applicant. (This section was included to provide feedback for students prior to their preemployment interviews.)

Comments:

A. Strengths:

B. Areas of concern:

C. Consider for future development:

D. Employability: Rate with 5 being the highest.

Scholarship	Unsatisfactory	1 2 3 4 5	Excellent
Appearance	Poor	1 2 3 4 5	Superior
Personality	Insecure	1 2 3 4 5	Poised
Educational knowledge	Diffused	1 2 3 4 5	Clear
Disposition	Negative	1 2 3 4 5	Cheerful/pleasant
Knowledge of basic instruction	Unsatisfactory	1 2 3 4 5	Knowledgeable
Knowledge of management	Unsure	1 2 3 4 5	Fully understood
Hiring recommendation	Do not consider	1 2 3 4 5	Hire or employ later

One unexpected occurrence during the portfolio presentations was the emotion that erupted as students shared not only their educational philosophies but their personal ones as well. Many students related that creating and presenting the portfolio was the most difficult thing they had ever done—not because of the time involvement, although that was substantial, but because of the self-evaluation required. They had finally reached a career climax, recognizing through their portfolio presentation all that they had accomplished.

One student said he or she actually slept with the portfolio at the end of the bed so it was the last thing thought about at night and the first thing thought about in the morning. The unique discovery of oneself begins as documents are collected, ideas are organized, philosophies reflected on, and artifacts presented (CORP). The lifelong journey of self-actualization has begun. Funny, it just looks like a notebook.

Summary

The assessment of portfolios is conducted through various means. Some of these are informal conversations with peers and faculty. Formal conferences also bring focus to portfolio progress and motivate the developer toward greater understanding. Checklists ensure that all components are included. Numerical or letter grades are given to assess levels of expertise. Rubrics are used as instructional tools as well as landmarks of growth. Likert-type scales also are used to accommodate the need for more standardized, objective methods of assessment.

The key is authentic assessment. Valid portfolio assessment must be flexible enough for each individual to include those artifacts that best represent one's teaching ability. Each individual's strengths and sophistication of thought along the journey should be validated. Variety and flexibility are needed for accurate examination. Professional dialogue about growth and development should be a by-product of portfolio development. And through the assessment, a shared vision of educators striving to meet goals of individual potential is forged.

7

Putting It All Together
Nuts and Bolts

"Okay," thought Juan, "I finally have the information I need to put this portfolio thing together." He had it, all right—in notebooks, in file folders, in boxes, and on disks. Some of the necessary documents were in the trunk of his car, and he still needed to retrieve some letters of recommendation from his former employers and public school mentors.

The physical component of the portfolio was something he had not thought about until recently. Now he wondered how to showcase the myriad artifacts he had collected. He did not want to carry a gigantic 10-pound notebook into the interviews, but he did want the interviewer to be impressed with his organization and ability. His portfolio was a physical documentary complementing his talent, his long-range commitment, and the progress he had made during the past few years. So, how was Juan going to bring all this information into some type of logical, well-defined employment tool?

"One thing is certain, Juan. You must have a plan, an outline for organization. Then, you have to purchase the needed materials that will enhance the documents. Next, you'll determine the intended look of the final product. Finally, you'll have to put it all together. Like assembling a puzzle, you'll do it one piece at a time," advised Mr. Savage.

Begin With an Outline

Putting a portfolio together is analogous to writing a research paper. One must begin with an outline. One must think about major headings, subheadings, and supporting details. One must consider the introduction, body, and conclusion because the entire portfolio document will be more convincing if it has a seamless communication purpose.

When attempting to validate an area, goal, or competency, begin by informing the reader of the goal. Insert personal reflections and anecdotes to orient a reader into the supporting documents that validate the accomplishment of the goal. An example of validating the area of assessment might include the following outline:

I.   Assessment

The teacher understands and uses a variety of assessment strategies to evaluate and modify the teaching/learning process ensuring the continuous intellectual, social, and physical development of the learner.

    A.   Philosophy of assessment—comparable to an introductory paragraph of a research paper

    B.   Teacher-made samples

    C.   Student work

    D.   Grade book sample

Begin with a major heading, such as *Assessment* or some other required competency. Next, write an introductory statement or philosophy that gently guides the reader into your thoughts about the subject. The other subheadings would be the individual artifacts that support that major assessment heading. Samples of a variety of teacher-made tests/assignments could expand your original philosophy about authentic assessment. Copies of assignments/tests, including your written comments to the student, might also document the importance of teacher feedback. Including a grade book sample would validate the importance of documentation skills, including dates, assignments, percentage weight of individual assignments, and other factors that influence student assessment. Because validation is so important, be sure that your points are congruent with your introductory paragraph. This will keep the reader's thoughts following along with yours.

Introductory Narrative Statement

The following is an introductory narrative submitted by Oklahoma student Kim Holton in her terminal portfolio:

When developing a curriculum and deciding how you will instruct your students, you must consider several factors. Are your students learning all you intended for them to learn? Are there other considerations or areas of the students' development that need to be evaluated? Assessment is not only closely connected to a curriculum (what we teach) and instruction (how we teach it), but it can be used to evaluate students' cooperative skills, effort, and motivation.

Whenever I developed a lesson, unit, or learning center, I had to consider how I would assess the students. I have found it to be most important not only to rely on paper-and-pencil tests, but also use other methods of assessment as well.

Some of the documentation that supports my strength in assessment includes the following: anecdotal records, checklists (both for individuals and cooperative groups), quizzes, rubrics, and even short activities to check for comprehension.

During my student teaching semester, I also had the opportunity to help students prepare portfolios. They were even given a self-evaluation on how well they thought they were learning. Writing notebooks were also kept in order to reflect the students' progress in their writing.

I believe that by utilizing a variety of assessment tools and keeping thorough records, teachers can better communicate to the parents the level of their child's maturity and academic success.

I have included the following pages in order to substantiate my competency in the area of assessment. The documents include these possibilities: a quiz which followed a week-long unit on Oklahoma, checklists (both individual and group), anecdotal notes, two rubrics used to evaluate student performance in my science learning center, daily oral language corrections, math fact assessment, and bulletin board cutouts used to assess whether or not the students understood the difference between facts and opinions.

Kim's introduction, philosophy of assessment, variety of assessment samples, and conclusion concisely reflect important ideas and artifacts. They demonstrate her ability to create, evaluate, and report assessing student progress. Her examples support her basic philosophy so an administrator can see that she "practices what she preaches."

Consideration of Physical Characteristics

There are several ways to compile information into a portfolio. Some portfolios are assembled on disk, on-line, or in paper, picture, or multimedia formats. Even if you have some electronic material that is interactive, such as a Web page with links to further information, or have additional materials on disk, be prepared to give the interviewer a paper copy with pertinent information. Having a table of contents or an outline with the on-line information, as well as a résumé, can provide necessary facts. Because most interviewers require a paper trail (district policies may require a copy of all applicants' résumés, applications be sent/housed in a central location), provide the evaluator or interviewer with a hard copy containing vital information such as a résumé and certification credentials.

Currently, however, some universities and businesses are accepting, or in some cases requiring, electronic versions that include video/audiotape with interactive components. Designing the portfolio to meet individual employment or scholastic purposes is vital. Keeping documents on disk, whether CD-ROM or floppy, ensures the longevity of the materials and affords flexibility when tailoring the portfolio for specific employers or courses.

Determination of Style

The approach of the portfolio should be a good fit with both your personality and the intended use of the portfolio. An artist's portfolio is expected to be creative, sophisticated, funky, or avant garde, whereas a portfolio for a business company will be formalized and follow prescribed conventional business practice in its presentation. The teaching portfolio should mirror your teaching preferences, philosophy, and style.

Paper Portfolios

Some standard physical components that can reflect individual style with a paper portfolio include the following:

Notebooks

Many teaching portfolios are collected in three-ring loose-leaf notebooks. They vary in thickness from 1" to 3", depending on the quantity of material in the portfolio collection, and are available in a variety of sizes, colors, and options. Some have plastic envelopes to accommodate disks and video- or audiotapes. Notebooks that have a plastic covering on the front, back, and spine foster individualization and continuity of design by allowing owner-designed insertions to be placed under the coverings. Loose-leaf notebooks are recommended because they allow one to insert pages where appropriate. Avoid notebooks with spiral binding because they limit flexibility if the student desires to change the format or style of the portfolio. Because the portfolio will become an organic documentation of growth, one needs the option of adding or deleting pages with minimal effort. Leather loose-leaf portfolios with engraved names/initials are also available, though more costly.

Use of Graphics, Photographs, and Borders

Be consistent in the use of borders and graphics throughout the entire portfolio. If a double-lined or preprinted border is used on the cover, then use the same one on divider pages throughout. Some students have used professionally manufactured papers with colorful borders for the divider pages and cover. This can be effective for elementary education portfolios, whereas secondary students may prefer a more business-like paper style. Whatever the chosen selection, continuity of design holds the information together and presents a polished, professional look.

Do not allow the graphics to become the focus of your portfolio. The document is not to be used as a bulletin board and administrators will not base employment on who has the "cutest" notebook. The portfolio will be presented in a professional setting, and the tone of the portfolio should reflect that environment.

When using photographs, rather than including the original, have a color reproduction made on the same paper to be used in the portfolio. This not only protects the original from being damaged but also allows positioning/sizing on the page with room for text captions identifying the photographs. This method allows the portfolio pages to remain flat with no protruding edges; such presentation offers a more professional look.

Type of Paper

Use a quality grade (22 pound or more) paper that is gentle on the eye. The overall goal of the portfolio is to have your audience motivated to read the information. A fluorescent lime-green paper, for instance, is not eye-appealing and will make the reader want to close the portfolio as soon as possible. Select a color that is both personally pleasing and has a professional look.

Purchasing plastic acetate sleeves in which to insert original artifacts both protects the original documents and allows easy movement of materials within the portfolio. The covers with three-hole edges also prevent having to use a hole punch when assembling materials. The time-saving factor alone justifies using them. Letters of recommendation, résumés, and other materials maintain their crisp, original, professional appearance. The covers also allow the reviewer to peruse the documents without fear of finger smudges or the inevitable tearing of holes punched directly into the artifact. The durability afforded by these plastic covers far outweighs their initial expense.

Type of Outside Cover

The outside cover of the portfolio resembles a title page. It should include a title for the portfolio, such as "Professional Portfolio," "Teaching Portfolio," "Educational Portfolio," or some other such appropriate heading. The next item on the cover should be the portfolio author's name. One may opt to add an address and telephone number as well at that juncture. Keep the cover simple and easy to read.

Font Type and Size

Because the portfolio is a professional document, the narratives included should be in standard 10- or 12-point type. Times New Roman font is easy to read and prints nicely, but any True Type font accepted by business standards is appropriate. When designing divider pages, create a template to keep all fonts, spaces, lines, and sizes uniform throughout the document.

The selection of font type and size should complement the paper/ graphic theme that you have selected. For example, an early childhood port- folio might have a border with children playing, so a childish scrawl font for dividers could fit in nicely with the overall look of the portfolio.

Method of Organization

Chronological. Depending on the type of portfolio, presenting documents in chronologies may be appropriate. If one is attempting to show growth for the developmental portfolio (see Chapter 2), then certainly this chronological approach would most likely be the method of organization—from "where I was" to "where I am." In this instance, one would begin with the event or document that initiated the need for growth and proceed to the highest and hopefully, current level of expertise. However, most résumés take the reverse approach, organizing documents within individual categories, with the most recent experience listed first and the past experience listed last.

The key, again, is consistency. Starting with the most recent, and follow- ing that prescribed method throughout allows the reader to follow the pro- gression in an orderly and sequential fashion.

Competency-based. Creating a portfolio based on specified competencies, goals, or standards is the frequent method of organization for educators. Be- cause the university or organization has specified plateaus of achievement (outcomes) that are expected, educators must prioritize materials with stan- dards driving the selection and documentation of materials.

In the list that follows, Interstate New Teacher Assessment and Support Consortium Standards beginning teacher requirements are mandated. This model has set standards for beginning teacher licensing and development. Using these standards, the portfolio must validate competency in each of the areas. When organizing the portfolio, each of the following categories must be included with supporting evidence to demonstrate skills. The general ap- proach is indicative of a showcase portfolio (see Chapter 3) with best works presented for each standard.

- Standard 1: Subject matter. The teacher understands the central con- cepts, tools of inquiry, and structures of the discipline(s) he or she teaches and can create learning experiences that make these aspects of subject matter meaningful for students.
- Standard 2: Student learning. The teacher understands how children and youths learn and develop and can provide learning opportunities that support their intellectual, social, and personal development.
- Standard 3: Diverse learners. The teacher understands how learners differ in their approaches to learning and creates instructional oppor- tunities that are adapted to learners from diverse cultural back- grounds and with exceptionalities.

- Standard 4: Instructional strategies. The teacher understands and uses a variety of instructional strategies to encourage the students' development of critical thinking, problem solving, and performance skills.

- Standard 5: Learning environment. The teacher uses an understanding of individual and group motivation and behavior to create a learning environment that encourages positive social interaction, active engagement in learning, and self-motivation.

- Standard 6: Communication. The teacher uses knowledge of effective verbal, nonverbal, and media communication techniques to foster active inquiry, collaboration, and supportive interaction in the classroom.

- Standard 7: Planning instruction. The teacher plans and manages instruction based on knowledge of subject matter, students, the community, and curriculum goals.

- Standard 8: Assessment. The teacher understands and uses formal and informal assessment strategies to evaluate and ensure the continuous intellectual, social, and physical development of his or her learners.

- Standard 9: Reflection and professional development. The teacher is a reflective practitioner who continually evaluates the effects of his or her choices and actions on others (students, parents, and other professionals in the learning community) and who actively seeks out opportunities to grow professionally.

- Standard 10: Collaboration, ethics, and relationships. The teacher communicates and interacts with parents/guardians, families, school colleagues, and the community to support the students' learning and well-being.

When corroborating skills in each area, include only pertinent documents that truly demonstrate expertise. Be selective about chosen materials. If one desires, a listing of other materials or an addendum that supports the competency can be saved in files on a floppy disk so a reviewer could retrieve them if needed. The documents on the disk should be arranged in the same order as they appear in the paper portfolio. Folders for each category or topic can be developed for ease both in retrieval and in adding further documents.

Importance to author. Some portfolio sections require or allow individual reflection about topics or artifacts within the standards. Although some of the thoughts will be directly integrated with the standards, sometimes a separate section entitled *Personal Accomplishments* can be inserted to include events that demonstrate personal growth that are not included elsewhere in the portfolio. From this construct, items that are most meaningful to the author would be listed first with appropriate reflections about why they were chosen for inclusion.

Mandated by organization. The first consideration when developing a portfolio is inclusion of every mandated item. Even within these required constructs, however, the individual has the opportunity to include documents of "best works" that fit the parameters of the organization's mandated items. For example, a résumé is almost always required in a portfolio. The individual, however, chooses not only what to include but how it will be arranged. The individuals then are given the opportunity of producing a résumé with the results set up in varying styles and designs.

Combination of methods. Portfolio organization may include one or more of the previously mentioned methods, or even another self-developed strategy that has proven effective. Within some categories, a chronology may work best. In other optional categories, you could showcase in some type of sequential order those artifacts important to you. Clarity and flow keep the reader involved, so regardless of the method, coordination should be evident. Combining two or more presentational styles may provide just the right vehicle for moving the samples along.

Captions

All photographs, student work samples, certificates, newspaper articles, personal notes, memorabilia, and other related materials supporting competencies must include captions. Do not assume that the reader will link the artifact (e.g., photograph of a baseball team) with a fact that you stated in your résumé (e.g., volunteer coach for three summers with the freshman baseball team).

Captions can be highlighted by a different colored text, a different colored paper, or with a colored highlighter. They should be clearly identified as a classifier for the artifact. Captions should include the five W's—who, what, when, where, and why. As in the previous example, one would include a caption similar to the following: "This artifact is a team photograph (what) of the Centerville, Iowa (where) freshman baseball team (who) that I coached during the summers of 1995-1998 (when). We played approximately 17 games, and I spent about 15 hours per week for 6 weeks working with the players. I felt it was important for me to learn the fundamentals of working with a group, and besides that, I learned some great lessons about dealing with parents" (why). The entire reflection and validation for the artifact would be a further expansion of the *why.*

Chosen Artifacts

The selection of artifacts is one of the most crucial areas in portfolio development. Hundreds of students must meet specific criteria, but how they choose to demonstrate the skills will determine the success or failure of their portfolio. When selecting documents or artifacts, include those that you can validate, justify, and support. Be prepared when an evaluator asks you specific questions such as, "How does this artifact demonstrate your under-

standing of the competency?" or "Why do you feel this artifact is the best representative of your skill in this area?" or "I don't see linkage between this document and the competency. Could you explain to me how they fit together?"

Imagine that you are on trial for having skill in a particular area such as
classroom management. Your included portfolio items should be enough
evidence to convict you. Do not rely on hearsay or circumstantial evidence,
but only on objective, cold, hard facts. These verify to the evaluator that you
truly understand the standard, and your documented "evidence" proves your
understanding beyond a shadow of doubt.

Ask a peer to review your materials to determine if he or she understands
the order, sequence, and content. Get feedback from various people, including experienced teachers and administrators. Portfolios are not to be created
in a vacuum. The more information and opinions you can garner from
sources outside yourself, the better the outcome will be. You must make the
ultimate choice, but weigh all suggestions from respected outside advisors.

Language

Obviously, the information included in the portfolio is important. The vehicle
by which the information is delivered is almost as important. The style of
language, sentence structure, introductory and closing paragraphs, spelling
accuracy, colorful words, analogies, and narrative clarity influence the evaluator's opinion about your level of development.

Some students have wonderful truckloads of skills, information, and experiences. Yet, having the cargo does not ensure delivery. Although running
the risk of redundancy, it bears repeating. Remember that all ideas and information must be error free. This means proofreading and rereading and having someone else read it again and again (see Resource E). Poorly constructed
sentences, weak grammar, or colloquialisms have no place in your employment or showcase portfolio. Just as the physical constructs of the portfolio
reflect who you are, so does your language.

Electronic Portfolios

This type of portfolio is becoming more and more popular for a number of
reasons. Terry Wiedmer (1998), an assistant professor in the Department of
Educational Leadership at Ball State University, elaborates:

> The use of electronic portfolios is gaining popularity as educators
> and business people alike are discovering their benefits as a means of
> validating individual performance. Aided by technology, individuals
> can develop portfolios by electronic means and create, store, and
> manage both products and processes for inclusion. . . . The new tech-
> nologies make it possible to show, in ways that were not available be-
> fore, what students and professionals working in the field know and
> can do. (p. 586)

Because the sheer number of portfolio artifacts can quickly accumulate into a massive amount of documentation, the floppy disk or CD-ROM not only adds additional storage in a small instrument, but also allows for quick editing. The added flexibility of being able to tailor individual disks for viewing by prospective employers or university evaluators provides an attractive option for busy job hunters.

Other pluses include the fact that scanning various documents saves time, and the video/audio components provide actual documentation of your teaching skills. Additionally, storage in this manner makes it viable for the user to document growth continually with minimal work. The electronic portfolio allows an additional option of submitting the portfolio to various businesses and educational systems on the World Wide Web. Again, time and expense are spared through the use of electronic media.

Because electronic portfolios use multimedia in presenting credentials, the applicant must determine if the reviewers will be willing to take the time to review the portfolio or have the equipment necessary for that reviewing. Because teaching requires skills other than putting together a "slick" multimedia presentation, administrators will be unlikely to hire an applicant based solely on the contents of the electronic portfolio. As in paper portfolios, administrators or interview committees are more receptive to an in-depth review after an applicant has successfully completed an interview and has been chosen as one of a few select applicants for further consideration.

Commercial Programs

Various commercial programs are currently being used in electronic portfolio development. Programs are designed for diverse users—from primary-age students to adults—and include applications that can be used by novices as well as computer techs. Some programs frequently mentioned in research include the following:

- The Grady Profile—Aurbach and Associates (800-774-7239)
- The Teacher's Portfolio derived from Grady Profile, especially designed for teaching professionals—Aurbach and Associates
- Portfolio Assessment Toolkit—Hyperstudio Companion Product that can be moved between Mac and Windows systems—Designer Software
- Learner Profile: Observational assessment tool—Sunburst/Wings for Learning (800-321-7511)
- HyperCard—Claris Corporation
- HyperStudio—Roger Wagner Productions
- Designer Portfolio Template for HyperStudio
- Electronic Portfolio—Scholastic
- The Teaching Pro—electronic portfolio service—K LeMair

- Chalkboard 1.0—Association of Supervision and Curriculum Development
- FileMaker Pro 3.0
- Newton
- Electronic Portfolio—Learning Quest, Inc. (541-753-6474)
- KidPix and KidPix Companion—Borderbund

Hardware Recommendations

Suggested minimum hardware needed for electronic portfolio production includes a standard computer, Iomega Zip Drive, Connectix Quick Cam, and a Visioneer Paper Port. Other nifty items are a microphone, camcorder, digital camera, audiocassette recorder, and a video compression board to input QuickTime movies.

Mining the Internet

There are numerous links (see Resource C) to portfolio development on the Internet. One can see examples of electronic portfolios, portfolio requirements from business and academic institutions, instructions for step-by-step construction of portfolios, research, newsletters, news groups, and commercial materials regarding portfolio development.

Before creating a portfolio, surf the Web and investigate some of the numerous sites. Good ideas abound, and one has the opportunity to review diverse types of portfolios, methods of presenting and organizing materials, and evaluation rubrics.

Advice on Getting Started: The Art of Ending Procrastination

Do it right or don't do it at all. A lousy self-presentation Web site will hurt you more than it will help you. *Lousy* includes: a Web site that rambles or repeats your résumé, spelling or grammatical errors, broken links, graphics that don't show up or are too "busy," and not knowing how to view the site on the interviewer's computer.

Start now. Better yet, start yesterday.

Your portfolio is a good start—but it's only a start. *Do not* just hand an interviewer your whole portfolio. You'll want to groom, edit, and reorganize selected portions of your portfolio for presentation.

Think about the content before you start worrying about design. List the 3 to 4 experiences you would most like to highlight. Write a paragraph or two about those experiences. Write them out in longhand, or type them on your computer.

Once you have your content ready to go, decide how your pages will link together.

Once you figure out how your pages will relate to each other, decide on the graphic elements: colors, pictures, background, and text layout.

Make one page with all the elements you need (graphics, header, footer, body text) and use it as a template (that is, to make a new page, open this page and choose "Save As . . . " from the file Menu). This will make all your pages look the same.

Upload your pages. Open the pages on a Mac and an IBM, using Netscape® and Internet Explorer®, if possible. Test all your links. Have your roommate test your links. Call friends at other colleges and have them test your links. One bad link might make your interviewer quit reading.

Print your pages out. Proofread them. Have your roommate proofread them. Take your page to the writing center and have them proofread them. Writing errors speak poorly of your abilities. (Kalamazoo College, 1998)

Many pages are available for consideration on portfolio development, some of which include a database of information about schools that are requiring or developing educational portfolios—no need to reinvent information that is public domain or easily adapted to suit individual needs.

Time and Money

Portfolios are not tests that can be crammed for the night before. Their very essence is one of longevity, growth, development, and experiential learning. Collecting and assembling the materials, whether paper or electronic, is a commitment in persistence and endurance. As with any project, you get out what effort you put in, or *junk in, junk out*. Because portfolios are teaching documentaries, they at times consume one's thoughts, choices, and time.

Begin now to save and document all your experiences. Collecting artifacts and thinking in terms of confirming activities is so much easier than trying to create an artificial scenario, or worse yet, having an undocumented experience, then trying to recreate the feelings and reactions of the moment. Because portfolios are representative of authentic assessment, the items included should be those events that naturally occur in your educational career. Therefore, the collection should become cyclic rather than a one-time mad dash prior to the portfolio due date.

Reflection is a difficult, thought-provoking journey. It takes us down through some valleys and up on a few mountain tops as well. A self-examination journey is not completed in a single night, but often takes weeks, months, and years. Portfolios that demonstrate that type of commitment and dedication are successful. The sense of pride of workmanship is exhibited from the paper to the Web page and all those documents in between. Because when a comprehensive collection is assembled, the portfolio becomes a mini-representation of you: it holds your thoughts, goals, achievements, and shortcomings.

The cost of an individual portfolio can vary from quite inexpensive to extravagant. Basic costs typically include a notebook ($5 to $10), acetate sleeves ($10 per hundred), ream of 22-pound paper ($7), divider insert pages ($2), tabs for dividers ($2), disk for storage ($1), miscellaneous printing costs ($5), and possibly video- or audiotapes ($7). Color reproductions of photographs can be costly if access to a scanner or digital camera is not available. The bottom line cost for a portfolio is generally from $30 to $50. That amount is not excessive when one considers that the volume becomes the keeper of your dreams.

Timeline of Portfolio Development

1. Collect and document all experiences. Save all returned assignments. Keep all evaluations of teaching, observing, and so forth. Take pictures of items or activities that would not "fit" in a traditional portfolio such as artwork, a teacher-created game/bulletin board, and working with students. Assemble in boxes, file folders, or on computer disks.
2. Determine what standards are to be met in the portfolio.
3. Select appropriate artifacts that support the standards.
4. Think about selected items. Talk to others about items and their appropriateness. Change if necessary.
5. Develop an outline of materials to include both mandatory and optional artifacts.
6. Think about your philosophies and write them down.
7. Determine the method of organization and develop a table of contents.
8. Put all materials together in file folders according to your outline/ table of contents.
9. Get feedback from others regarding the contents.
10. Proofread. Proofread. Proofread.
11. Assemble everything as a professional product.
12. Prepare for presentation.
13. Share the portfolio with others.
14. Keep adding to your "self-portrait" of documentation.

8

Presenting the Professional Portfolio

The portfolio was complete, the pictures in their proper place with appropriate headings. The philosophies were written, the lesson plans prepared, and the evaluations complete. Now Jerry was ready to present his portfolio and prepare for his first job interview.

He wanted to appear confident, but he did not want to come across as a braggart. He had no idea what type of questions he would be asked. Actually, he was scared stiff about the whole process of interviewing and writing letters of application. He knew that if he made one error, the human resource director might just chuck his application and résumé into File 13. Jerry wanted to follow the proper guidelines, but how would he know the accepted process in each district?

He had heard some students talk about the legality of some questions and wondered what his rights were. What if the interviewer asked a question to which he did not know the answer? Should he fake it or just admit his stupidity? And how was he going to use his portfolio to the best advantage? Jerry had heard some principals say they did not want huge notebooks filling up their offices, so was all this portfolio work down the tubes?

Jerry hoped that by the time he walked into an interview, some of these questions would be answered.

The First Step in Presentation

After the portfolio is compiled, the presentation begins. Initial portfolio presentation may begin as a professor reviews it with a student, or as it is shared with a group of educators. In a university setting, an oral presentation is often required to meet specified program or course requirements. In an employment setting, the presentation interfaces with a job interview and determines the offer of employment.

No matter what the setting, the presentation is a vital part of the portfolio process. There are some basic presentational skills that can be used when sharing the portfolio with others. When applying for a teaching job, understanding the interview process and generic etiquette expectations can ease the apprehension new graduates experience. Understanding the legalities regarding employment practices can also boost your confidence because of the knowledge you will be treated fairly and equitably.

Although some areas overlap, this text will begin with the presentation of an undergraduate student presenting to a professor or committee and then proceed to presenting for employment, and further, tenure purposes.

Preparing for the Presentation

Once the portfolio is ready for the first oral presentation, then one is ready to share it with others. The following are some items to consider before presenting:

1. Who will be evaluating the presentation? Use examples that will validate your unique skills and also satisfy a specific audience.
2. What criteria will be used to evaluate? If possible, obtain a copy of the rubric or evaluation scale to be used. Be meticulous about including all required items, meeting or exceeding the acceptable level.
3. What is the time frame of the presentation? Never exceed the allotted time. Practice. Rehearse. Know your material, and prove to your audience your knowledge and expertise.
4. Will the format be strictly a presentation, or will there be a forum for questions? Try to anticipate what questions will be asked, what your responses will be, and how the portfolio artifacts demonstrate your skills.
5. Has an outline been prepared? Having the basic points on a card demonstrates your ability to plan. And even if you do not use it, such a guide provides a safety net for nervousness, forgetfulness, or side-tracking.
6. Does your apparel and grooming reflect the seriousness of this professional presentation? Wear something comfortable and attractive. Poise and a self-confident attitude enhance any presentation.
7. Is the presentation free of slang and grammatical errors? Be cognizant of the fact that you will be judged by what you say and how you say it. A poor oral presentation will sabotage an exceptional portfolio. If you currently use colloquialisms and slang, begin now to correct these to a standard form of English. Formal occasions require formal speech.
8. Have you rehearsed the physical logistics of finding materials in the portfolio quickly and "upside down?" Those evaluating the portfolio will want to actually see what is included, so the presenter, out of def-

erence to the viewer, will be showing the material by looking at it up-side down. There is an art to sharing the information included in a notebook format, but it takes some practice (see the portfolio oral pre-sentation evaluation in Chapter 6).

Preparing for the Interview

Actually, preparing for an interview begins with your initial contact with the school. Schools are contacted in various ways such as the following:

a. Telephone
b. Job fair/recruitment seminar
c. Letter
d. Application
e. Personal visit

When contacting a school for possible employment, follow standard rules of employment etiquette. Finding out who to contact, when to contact, and how frequently to remain in touch are just a few of the nuances that can impact your chances of employment. If unsure about the proper procedures, call the central administration office and ask for the secretary. Application forms, telephone numbers, names, titles, and sequence of employment pro-cedures can be obtained and are generally available in written form in an employment packet.

Be Nice to the School Secretary

Often, the first person you will meet will be the school secretary. Do not un-derestimate the influence of a secretary's opinion. If you are rude, then chances are your rudeness will be remembered. If you are courteous and pro-fessional, that will be noted as well. Polish your telephone skills and greet each person with whom you speak with respect and courtesy. Keep the con-versation pleasant but businesslike. State the request; thank the person; hang up. Because you hope to be gainfully employed at the school, do not blow it by being too nosy, too talkative, or too pushy.

Do Your Homework

Aha! Thought you were through with that, didn't you? It is not over yet. When applying at a school, learn all you can about the school. Investigate. Talk to people in the community. Read the local newspapers, or better yet, read the school newsletters. If possible, obtain a copy of a student or teacher hand-book. Familiarize yourself with the policies and procedures of the district. Many districts have this information on the World Wide Web, so check it out.

Knowing the expectations of the school can assist you in tailoring your responses to meet their guidelines.

Becoming a chameleon is not the advice here. However, if the district guidelines fit nicely with your educational philosophy, then certainly highlight that fact during the interview. The key is preparedness. Knowing that a district, for example, prohibits corporal punishment would certainly be pertinent to a question such as "What type of discipline plan will you implement in your classroom?" Do not dig a hole from which you cannot jump out. You may also wish to adjust your portfolio's discipline philosophy to correlate with the district's guidelines.

Similarly, your knowledge about specific educational programs regarding curriculum, extracurricular activities, and other important areas also serves as springboards during the interview. It is important to be able to articulate your educational philosophies, but familiarize yourself with the local backdrop from which you speak. "Know thyself," but also know thy prospective school district's policies.

What to Wear

Although most people spend an inordinate amount of time deciding what outfit to wear for an interview, the rules are relatively simple. A color consultant told a group of students that they should definitely wear something that (a) makes them feel good, (b) has garnered compliments, (c) looks as good seated as it looks standing, (d) is appropriate for the particular organization, and (e) has a polished "air" about it.

Some appearance/grooming faux pas during an educational interview include the following: too much aftershave or perfume (with all the allergies today, play it safe and stick to soap and water); too much jewelry (keep it simple); long, brightly colored nails (have them well-manicured but average length); unpolished shoes (people notice); outrageous hair styles (we are talking purple, extreme spikes, or words shaved in); spiked heels (how would you teach in those anyway?); open-toed shoes (it is not the beach); low-cut blouses or shirts (do not let them see anything below your collarbone); jeans or shorts (too casual); and generally, anything that would detract or cause attention to be deflected from you and what you have to say. Most educational organizations are still relatively conservative. Your persona should reflect your awareness of that fact.

Most schools require standard professional attire for men and women. Men typically are safe with a dress shirt, slacks, tie, and sports jacket. For a very formal district, a suit may be the norm. Women can choose to wear a suit, a tailored dress/jacket, or a pantsuit. Some very formal districts would frown on the pantsuit, but again, know the district's policy. If unsure, ask the secretary or a teacher in the district what constitutes acceptable interviewing attire. Given the choice of being too conservative or too liberal, opt for the first. No eyebrows will be raised from this option.

Detracting Behaviors

Certainly this is not a complete listing, but school administrators and personnel directors are just people. Here are few things that cause them to push their "Reject" buttons. "Avoid these," you know, "like the plague!"

1. Chewing gum (same applies to hard candies and mints or anything that impairs your speech).
2. Giving a limp handshake (look people in the eye and have a firm but not crushing grip).
3. Entering the office and plopping down (remember what your mother taught you—wait to be invited in and to be seated).
4. Smelling of smoke (avoid that last cigarette in the parking lot).
5. Calling the interviewer by their first name (use the correct title: Mr., Miss, Mrs., Ms., or Dr.).
6. Using nonstandard speech as well as slang (good or poor habits will help or haunt you here).
7. Being too nonchalant (insert enthusiasm and energy into comments).
8. Asking inappropriate questions (e.g., "Do I get the job?").
9. Being too casual (do not make yourself at home, it is not your office).

Enhancing Behaviors

1. Being on time (5 to 10 minutes early helps).
2. Being courteous to all school personnel.
3. Smiling; displaying a sense of humor.
4. Demonstrating a knowledge of state and national standards and the ability to address them in daily lessons.
5. Acknowledging the importance of technology and a willingness to integrate it into classroom practice.
6. Showing an ability to think through a complex question before answering.
7. Having some knowledge of the school district policies and programs.
8. Asking intelligent questions.
9. Displaying sincerity, genuineness, and enthusiasm.
10. Answering honestly posed questions, not "canned" answers.
11. Having poise and confidence despite nervousness.
12. Acknowledging a "willingness to try" attitude.
13. Being an unselfish team player.
14. Showing flexibility and adaptability.

15. Being willing to make mistakes to achieve a greater goal; an adventurous and curious spirit.

16. Acknowledging a strong work ethic.

17. Recognizing the importance of lifelong learning.

18. Being prepared and organized.

19. Demonstrating reflective thoughts about personal progress.

20. Displaying a grateful spirit for those who have helped you along the way; also, a handwritten thank-you note following the interview will be positively received.

The interview is undoubtedly the single most important element in getting hired. However, many students will never even reach this level in the hiring process because previous documents were not in proper order. The résumé and letter of application are vital in "getting your foot in the door." If these are poorly done, you may never even reach the interview stage. It is vital that you create a résumé that is error free, easy to read, highlights your skills, and captures the attention of the reviewer.

The Résumé

A good résumé is one to two pages in length, and concisely provides a minisnapshot of your career goals, education, and work experience. It should include the following information: name, address, e-mail address, and telephone number; career objective; education (degrees, certificates, specialized training, accomplishments); work experience (military, paid/volunteer skills, tutoring, substitute teaching, professional development activities); professional memberships (offices held, honors, committees, speaker, panel member); and references (name, phone number, address, job title). An honors or accomplishment section can be added to highlight outstanding achievement. If a placement file is available, include the name of the university, contact person, and telephone number.

All dates should be arranged chronologically from most recent to least recent. For a college graduate, include only recent activities: those that have occurred since high school graduation. Work experience could extend further into the past to show work history patterns. The language used to validate educational experiences should enhance your skills. A list of descriptive words is included in Resource A.

The physical format of the résumé can be used to attract a reader's attention. Use spacing, boldface type, columns, and fonts to your advantage. Keep it simple, easy to read, and consistent throughout. Select a color and style of paper that complements the print. This is not the place to be creative with preprinted borders or neon colors. Use standard business colors such as white, off-white, or pale gray. Purchase paper that is at least 22-pound weight. This means that it is substantial (cannot see through it, and is not slick like typing paper), feels good in the reader's hand, does not tear easily, and shouts of good taste and class. Pay the extra money necessary for fine résumé-type paper and matching envelopes.

The entire résumé should be error free. One mistake, and the document could end up at the bottom of the pile. Draft friends and colleagues to proofread the résumé and make suggestions about the format. This one document can greatly enhance your chances for getting an interview. Make sure the résumé begs to be read by being letter perfect, attractive, and packed with pertinent information.

Letter of Application

Often, applicants are required to submit a letter of application for each position they are seeking. When composing the letter, use the first paragraph to introduce yourself to the principal/employment officer. If you know the specific position for which you are applying, include where you saw the vacancy listing; otherwise, compose a general letter of application. The second paragraph should include specific information correlating with the requirements in the vacancy listing or advertisement. If specific criteria are not met, then state what other experiences you have had that would substitute for those skills. The final paragraph should express a desire to visit further about your credentials and your willingness to schedule an interview (include your phone number). A simple thank-you and résumé/application enclosure concludes the letter. Always use standard business format: address the letter to the appropriate person, double-check for grammar and spelling errors, and use a traditional font with 10- or 12-point size of type.

William S. Frank's CareerLab® (1998) lists some common letter-writing mistakes including the following: addressing letters "Dear Sir"(keep it gender free), no signature, spelling/grammar errors, handwritten letters (unless a brief thank-you note), using the word "I" too much, faxing a letter when the person is not expecting it, too many "creative" fonts and sizes, stifled wording, letters too long or too short, abbreviating words, using substandard business format, forgetting to include a résumé after stating it was enclosed, and sentences that are too long (like this one!).

Frequently Asked Questions

Although each principal/human relation's officer tailors specific questions to the district's needs and goals, many questions are typically asked during a teacher interview. These questions can be grouped around such categories as the National Council for Accreditation of Teacher Education Standards, including (a) development, learning, and motivation; (b) curriculum; (c) instruction; (d) assessment; and (e) professionalism. Or they can include, as the Interstate New Teacher Assessment and Support Consortium's Model Standards for Beginning Teachers indicate, (a) subject matter, (b) student learning, (c) diverse learners, (d) instructional strategies, (e) learning environment, (f) communication, (g) planning instruction, (h) assessment, (i) reflection and personal development, and (j) collaboration, ethics, and relationships. The interviewee can expect a considerable amount of overlapping of the various areas and should be prepared to provide practical application as well as theoretical knowledge of the educational categories. The following sections include questions that are a sampling of interview questions one might encounter (Interview Experts, 1998; University of Colorado, 1998; see also College of William & Mary, 1996).

General Questions

- Tell me about yourself.
- Why do you want to become a teacher?
- What are your strengths? Weaknesses?
- With so many qualified applicants, why should I hire you rather than someone else?
- What do you expect of an administrator?
- What can you contribute to our school?
- What is the responsibility of public schools?
- How would your friends describe you?
- Describe yourself using five adjectives.
- Describe your working relationship with your cooperating teacher.
- What is the name of the latest professional book or article you have read that was not required reading? What prompted you to select this particular book/article?
- What is the greatest challenge for teachers today?
- What is your philosophy of education? assessment? parent involvement?

Classroom Management

- How do you feel about retaining students?
- What is the cause of most discipline problems?
- Describe your student teaching successes and failures.
- What is one accomplishment of which you are particularly proud? Why?
- Describe a perfect teacher.

Development, Learning, and Motivation

- What other experiences, besides classroom teaching, have you had working with children/youth?
- What obstacles have you overcome while attaining your teaching degree?
- Why did you choose to become a teacher?

- What qualities do you possess that will enable you to become an effective teacher?
- Why do you want to teach in our district?
- What type of planning is necessary to teach a lesson?
- How will you determine the sequence of skills that are to be taught?
- Have you developed a unit of study that was not in the text? If so, how did you determine the objectives?
- Does your college transcript adequately reflect your knowledge base? Why or why not?
- How does motivation impact learning?
- Do you consider yourself an organized person? Would your friends agree? Your college professors?
- What subjects/grade levels do you feel most comfortable teaching?
- What experiences have you had working with a diverse population?
- Do you use computers/Internet on a regular basis for personal use? Why or why not?
- What is your personal teaching vision statement?

Curriculum

- Describe how you would integrate our state learner outcomes/standards in your classroom.
- How will you develop a curriculum that is motivating for students?
- How will you meet the individual skills needs of students in your class?
- What makes a lesson successful for the learners?
- What things do you consider when planning lessons?
- How would you integrate technology into lessons?
- Tell me about some specialized learning programs with which you are familiar.
- What are the basic parts of any lesson you teach?

Instruction

- If I walked into your classroom, what would I see?
- How does the physical environment of a classroom enhance/detract from learning?
- What is your preferred teaching style?
- When would you use individualized, small-group/whole-group teaching approaches? Why?
- Describe an activity when you used cooperative groups.
- How do you maximize "time on task" in your classroom?

- What are some classroom rules that you like?
- What role does homework play in your class?
- What graphic organizers have you used when presenting lessons?
- What different teaching strategies have you used that have been successful?
- Explain the elements of effective instruction.
- How do you keep students on track during a classroom discussion?
- Do you think interdisciplinary learning has merit? Why or why not?
- What are some techniques you have used to motivate students to learn?
- Has inclusion of special education students helped or hurt the regular classroom?

Assessment

- Is it ever appropriate to give a student an F grade?
- While teaching a 2-week unit, describe some assessment techniques you might use.
- How will you communicate students' progress to parents?
- How would you prepare students for taking a standardized test?
- Name some various types of grading plans. Which ones do you feel are most effective? Why?
- How will you evaluate your own teaching effectiveness?
- What percentage of your class do you think will fail?
- Have you designed a performance or behavioral objective for a class? If so, what prompted you to do so?
- What steps would you take before recommending a student be screened for special-education evaluation services?
- How would you design a rubric to evaluate a specific classroom skill?
- Do you keep anecdotal records on student behavior/performance? If so, how do you manage them?
- What are the strengths/weaknesses of norm-referenced tests?
- After giving a test, you discover that more than half of the students have failed. What would you do?
- What type of questions do you include on a unit test? True/False? Multiple choice? Short answer? Discussion?

Classroom Management

- Describe your discipline plan and how you would implement it.
- What rules do you like to use in your classroom?

- Suppose a student broke one of those rules, what are some appropriate consequences for breaking that rule?
- How would you communicate classroom expectations to parents?
- Tell me about a difficult confrontation you had with a student and how you resolved it.
- What factors contribute to an excellent classroom environment?
- Name some nonverbal ways you can "quiet" a classroom.
- What would you do if a student continues to challenge you with disruptive behavior?
- What role does the teacher play in establishing a productive learning climate?
- When would you definitely send a student to the principal?

Professionalism

- What things will you do to ensure continued professional growth?
- How will you develop healthy interpersonal relations with your colleagues?
- Are you a member of professional organizations? If so, which ones?
- Do you subscribe to professional journals and magazines? Name them.
- What things will you do to earn the respect of your students, parents, and peers?
- What steps will you take to ensure parent involvement in our schools?
- Visualize teachers who are real "professionals." What characteristics do they have? What do they say? Do? Look like? What are they involved in?
- How will you demonstrate respect for the diverse cultures within your classroom?
- What would you like for students to say about their classroom experience with you as their teacher? What do you hope is your teaching legacy?
- Discuss ethics in the educational setting.

Elementary School Questions

- What reading/math programs have you experienced? (basal, phonetic, Saxon)
- Why would knowledge about child development cause you to reflect about appropriate instruction from Pre-K through fourth grade?
- What is an appropriate discipline plan for kindergarten? (insert grade-level vacancy)

- Explain how you might teach a "Frog Unit" across the curriculum.

Middle School Questions

- Why do you think so few teachers select the middle school as their first choice of teaching assignment?
- What are some characteristics unique to middle school students?
- Do you think middle school students would learn more or less working in small groups? Justify your answer.

Secondary School Questions

- What is an acceptable failure rate in high school courses? Explain.
- How would you engage high school students in learning?
- Justify to a parent your homework policy.

Situational Questions

In conjunction with general questions, administrators invariably use some situational questions. The same question is posed to all interviewees and then evaluated. The following scenarios are representative of a situational-type question:

- You discover that one of your students has been cheating on her homework. How do you respond?
- A student who has been labeled as a "troublemaker" has been re-assigned to your class. What do you do?
- What would you do if you discovered that a teacher in your building was having a sexual relationship with a student?

These open-ended questions are difficult to prepare for because they are designed to evaluate how well you "think on your feet" (UNL Web Server, 1998). It is important not to rush ahead to a quick-fix answer. Take time to contemplate and consider all facets of the situation before you speak.

Questions for the Interviewee to Ask

Once you have completed the "grilling" by an individual or committee, it is time for the last question: "Do you have any questions you'd like to ask us?" Be prepared. Now is the time to really shine and demonstrate that you have seriously thought about your teaching role. By asking pertinent questions, you can clarify any fuzzy areas and show that you understand the full spectrum of teaching responsibilities.

Applicants who plan questions prior to the interview, according to the Association for School and University Staffing, Inc. (Career Development Center, 1998), can give the interview team an idea about their knowledge of educational issues. They also provide an opportunity to expand your philosophy and share any special expertise you may have. Because the interview is a two-way street, the questions you ask will not only provide a clearer image of who you are but also arm you with the necessary information to determine if this position is one that you really want. Ask in order to find out. Tailor these questions to meet your individual needs, but keep them as brief as possible.

- What types of media resources are available?
- What reading/math programs are currently used?
- What school counselors or public agencies are available to help students and teachers?
- Are there districtwide student standards or exit outcomes?
- Will I need additional training to implement existing programs?
- Does the school have a computer lab, individual computers in each classroom, or both?
- Are classes self-contained or departmentalized?
- How much flexibility does the teacher have in regard to curriculum and instruction plans for each individual classroom?
- What are the staff development requirements/opportunities for your district?
- Does your district support full inclusion of special education students?
- What is the district's plan for remediating students?
- What special provisions are granted for gifted and talented students?
- Have any of the schools in this district been listed as *at risk*? Which ones?
- What support is given to beginning teachers in your district?
- What is the ratio of beginning teachers to experienced teachers?
- Tell me about the parent-teacher organization in the district.
- What parent/community volunteer programs are available?
- Describe the student composition in this school.
- Does the staff socialize outside the school setting?
- With what community affairs/organizations do the teachers become involved?
- Is involvement in the local teachers' organization mandatory or optional?
- What responsibilities, other than teaching, will I have during the school day? After school hours?
- What functions does the school/community expect me to attend?

- Are there fundraising requirements if I agree to sponsor a club?
- Approximately how many hours a week will this responsibility include?
- Will I be compensated for this activity, or is it considered a part of my regular teaching duties?
- Will I be working alone, or will another staff member be assigned to the same activity?

Legality of Questions

There are many questions that are legally asked of applicants, but there are some that are considered an infringement on individual rights or could be construed as prejudicial. Some questions that are not legal include the following:

1. Are you a U.S. Citizen?
2. Were you born in the U.S.?
3. What is your "native tongue"?
4. How old are you?
5. Are you married or divorced?
6. How many children do you have?
7. Have you ever been arrested?
8. What is your religious affiliation?

Keep in mind that although these questions are illegal, some district applications still ask applicants to list their birth date, race, marital status, and other personal information. You may opt to leave these items blank or insert "N/A" if you do not wish to divulge that information. You also have the option of politely refusing to answer an illegal question that is posed by stating "I'd rather not answer that question."

Presenting Your Portfolio During the Interview

Although much has been written about creating a portfolio, very little information is available for using the portfolio during the job interview. Previous applicants indicate that most interview committees and administrators were very impressed by the applicants' portfolios. Heather Augustine, Kansas State University graduate, states,

Although a portfolio was not required at the interviews, my superintendent informed me (after hiring me) that my portfolio played a big part in my getting hired because she could see specific examples of how I taught. . . . I had included a number of interdisciplinary units and lessons so she could see that I would be an interdisciplinary teacher. This was more effective than just saying "I use all subject areas in my curriculum."

Integrate Your Portfolio Throughout the Interview

During the interview, a wide variety of questions will be asked. As you answer the questions, use your portfolio as you would when teaching a lesson. Show specific portfolio documents to expand your answer or demonstrate your understanding of a specific skill. Do not wait until the end of the interview to ask, "Would you like to see my portfolio?" By then, the interview is concluded, and the committee is typically on a tight time schedule. Use your portfolio as a tool, an extension to elaborate or verify your understanding.

Jean Federico, Florida teacher, confirms that she got her job because she effectively used her portfolio throughout the interview.

I had my portfolio with me, and as soon as I was asked a question that was demonstrated in my portfolio, I opened the book and showed the pages as I talked. Then, I left the book open on the table in front of me. Two things happened—first, the presence of my portfolio served as a "security blanket" for me. Anytime I got nervous, I just had to glance at the book to remind myself that "I am ready for this interview and this job." Second thing—by the time the interview was over, the people sitting around the table were practically bursting with curiosity to see what was in the rest of the book.

Administrative Uses of Teaching Applicants' Portfolios

According to the University of Northern Iowa's (1998) on-line portfolio handbook, there are three ways that prospective employers use portfolios: (a) They do not require one and do not wish to see one, (b) they do not require one but will look at documents as presented by the applicant, and (c) they require one to validate your teaching ability.

"Fostering Teacher Growth From Within" by Carolyn Bunting (1997), advises that administrators may also use a beginning teacher's portfolio as a part of the initial screening process, to further prioritize applicants who appear equally qualified, and to use as a baseline for ongoing professional growth. "Hiring a New Teacher? Ask for a Portfolio," written by Robert Boody and Carmen Montecinos (1997), emphasizes the positives of administrative use of portfolios as "direct evidence of actual classroom performance" and "a concrete basis for insightful screening and interviewing" (p. 34).

Although some applicants will obtain a job without a portfolio, others believe that portfolios are becoming vital instruments in securing employment. As one colleague stated in an e-mail message, "If a student comes in without a portfolio, you wonder about them." Regardless of requirements, interview committees will be impressed with a well-organized professional portfolio. Because research indicates that a portfolio is most likely to be requested during a follow-up interview with the building principal, finalists need something to separate them from the rest of the pack. A portfolio affords that advantage.

Resources

Resource A
Descriptive Words To Enhance
Education-Related Activities

Personal Traits

enthusiastic	optimistic	adaptable	flexible	energetic
diplomatic	courteous	sincere	honest	punctual
conscientious	methodical	reliable	supportive	friendly
poised	helpful	unselfish	polite	creative
reflective	persistent	motivated	independent	encouraging
patient	gentle	assertive	dependable	intelligent

Leadership Traits

organized	directed	collected	assembled	modeled
planned	arranged	advised	listened	surveyed
assessed	delivered	volunteered	corrected	reflected
provided	assisted	coordinated	created	drafted
assigned	protected	prepared	demonstrated	supervised
recruited	hosted	supported	trained	tutored

Lifelong Learning Traits

curious	eager	self-directed	innovative	excited
challenging	participating	learning	improving	developing
stimulating	motivated	analyzing	expressing	studying
assisting	changing	accepting	seeking	considering

Resource B
Oklahoma General Competencies for Teacher Licensure and Certification

(Note: Adopted May 23, 1996, by the State Board of Education as required by Legislative House Bill 1549 for creation of a competency-based teacher preparation program to be implemented July 1, 1997.)

1. The teacher understands the central concepts and methods of inquiry of the subject matter discipline(s) he or she teaches and can create learning experiences that make these aspects of subject matter meaningful for students.

2. The teacher understands how students learn and develop, and can provide learning opportunities that support their intellectual, social, and physical development at all grade levels including early childhood, elementary, middle level, and secondary.

3. The teacher understands that students vary in their approaches to learning, and creates instructional opportunities that are adaptable to individual differences of learners.

4. The teacher understands curriculum integration processes and uses a variety of instructional strategies to encourage students' development of critical thinking, problem solving, performance skills, and effective use of technology.

5. The teacher uses best practices related to motivation and behavior to create learning environments that encourage positive social interaction, self-motivation, and active engagement in learning, thus providing opportunities for success.

6. The teacher develops knowledge of and uses communication techniques to foster active inquiry, collaboration, and supportive interaction in the classroom.

7. The teacher plans instruction based on curriculum goals, knowledge of the teaching/learning process, subject matter, students' abilities and differences, and the community, and adapts instruction based on assessment and reflection.

8. The teacher understands and uses a variety of assessment strategies to evaluate and modify the teaching/learning process ensuring the continuous intellectual, social, and physical development of the learner.

9. The teacher evaluates the effects of his or her choices and actions on others (students, parents, and other professionals in the learning community), modifies those actions when needed, and actively seeks opportunities for continued professional growth.

10. The teacher fosters positive interaction with school colleagues, parents/families, and organizations in the community to actively engage them in support of students' learning and well-being.

11. The teacher will have an understanding of the importance of assisting students with career awareness and the application of career concepts to the academic curriculum.

12. The teacher understands the process of continuous lifelong learning, the concept of making learning enjoyable, and the need for a willingness to change when the change leads to greater student learning and development.

13. The teacher understands the legal aspects of teaching including the rights of students and parents/families, as well as the legal rights and responsibilities of the teacher.

14. The teacher understands and is able to develop instructional strategies/plans based on the Oklahoma core curriculum.

15. The teacher understands the state teacher evaluation process, "Oklahoma Criteria for Effective Teaching Performance," and how to incorporate these criteria in designing instructional strategies.

Primary Source of Competencies

- Competencies 1 through 10 are based on "Model Standards for Beginning Teacher Licensing and Development: A Resource for State Dialogue," prepared by the Council for Chief State School Officers' Interstate New Teacher Assessment and Support Consortium.

- Competencies 11 through 13 were developed as a result of input from Oklahoma educators.

- Competencies 14 and 15 are based on Oklahoma law.

Representation of development committee: elementary teachers including Teacher of the Year finalists, elementary principals, and professors of teacher education.

Sources: Information from the National Council for Accreditation of Teacher Education (NCATE), Elementary Education Task Force, and Oklahoma's Core Curriculum Pursuant to 70 0.5 11-106.6 § a.

Resource C
On-Line Resources for the Development of Teacher Portfolios

National Standards/Goals

- President's and Secretary of Education's Priorities—All national initiatives and links to resources and documents. A must for educators. http://www.ed.gov/inits.html

- National Board for Professional Teaching Standards—Seeking National Board Certification—FAQ's, Talk to Other Teachers, General Information—The Standards: What Teachers Should Know and Be Able to Do. http://nbpts.org/nbpts/standards

- Association of Teacher Educators: Standards for Teacher Educators—Includes list of standards, indicators, evidence supporting proficiency, and assessment modes. http://www.siu.edu/departments/coe/ate/atestand.html

- National Council for Accreditation of Teacher Education—NCATE Constituent Membership—Links to each coalition membership group including organizations representing teacher educators, teachers, policy makers, subject specific areas, and others. http://www.ncate.org/general/conslist.html

- NCATE Standards—Contains the standards and indicators. http://www.ncate.org/about/stdintro.html

Portfolio Development

- The Kalamazoo Portfolio—Site designed for students to learn about it, create it, and use it; contains a database of institutions using portfolios; sample portfolios online. http://www.kzoo.edu/pfolio/

- Portfolio Checklist—Comprehensive list for student portfolio development. http://www.seattleu.edu/gerhold/portfolio.html

- Portfolios in Education—Includes numerous links to electronic portfolios, organizations, and student and teaching portfolios. http://www.uno.edu/edci/portfoli.htm

- Teaching Portfolios—Resource list, articles about documenting teaching, advantages of portfolios, uses and abuses. http://ublib.buffalo.edu/libraries/projects/tlr/development.html

- The Teaching Portfolio—Harriet W. Sheridan Center for Teaching and Learning. Includes introduction, format, procedures, and sample teaching portfolios. http://sheridan-enter.stg.brown.edu/publications/TeachingPortfolio.html

- Professional Portfolio Development Guide—Outstanding source for development including comprehensive appendix guidelines. Hard copy available for purchase. http://www.edu.uleth.ca/fe/ppd/contents.html

- Electronic Portfolio Bookmarks—Extensive list of links including a wide variety of topics. http://www.mtnbrook.k12.al.us/bwf/mumms/eportf2.htm

- Multimedia Portfolio Project—Resource for creating a multimedia portfolio with templates and training handouts. http://alive.gallaudet.edu/mmfolio/index.htm

- Sample Electronic Portfolios on the Net—Includes student and pre-service student portfolio projects, and on-line listserv. http://www.umcs.maine.edu/orono/collaborative/spring/electpor.html

- Resources: Budget and staff development for electronic portfolios. From Alaska, a barebones look at hardware, software, and other materials needed. http://www.uaa.alaska.edu/ed/portfolios/matrix.html

- Teaching Portfolios: Web links—Variety of sources for planning and assessing portfolios. http://fls.cll.wayne.edu/fls/teachptf.htm

- Awesome Library: Teacher Portfolios—Provides information about types of portfolios, electronic portfolios, and guidelines for creating and using them. http://www.awesomelibrary.org/Office/Teacher/Assessment_Information/Portfolios.htm

Job Search Resources

- Finding a Job: The New Teacher Page—Great link with resources, portfolio information, interview, résumé, and salary. http://www.geocities.com/~newteach

- A to Z New Teacher Stuff—Wonderful site with advice on interviews, portfolio building, and questions to ask. http://www.geocities.com/atozteachstuff/stuff/subsites.html

- Career Services Center Guide to Interview Questions for Educators—Contains 17 typical questions for elementary and secondary teachers. http://www.usfca.edu/usf/career

- School District Interview Questions for Teachers—Is just what the title says, very practical with interviewing tips from University of Colorado at Denver. http://www.cudenver.edu/

- Interview Experts: Your Career Resource Center—Extremely helpful site includes interview questions, illegal questions, résumé construction, cover letters, dress, and behavior. http://www.interviewexperts.com/index.htm

- Questions to Ask in Education Interviews: Career Development Center—Lists questions the interviewee should ask before taking the job. http://www.snybuf.edu/cdc/resume/eduques.htm

Resource D
Portfolio Planner

Student Name: Date:

Conferences Number:

Competency/standard (list one per sheet):

Evidence/documentation (include as many artifacts as required):

Artifact 1 (list):

    Theory/rationale/reflection:

    Application:

Artifact 2 (list):

    Theory/rationale/reflection:

    Application:

Other possible artifacts:

Artifacts need to obtain before next conference:

Resource E
Portfolio Quality Checklist

This is a checklist designed to assist students in producing a quality portfolio. Ask the following questions prior to portfolio submission:

- Do the contents provide a clear summary of student's experiences in the program and what was learned from them?
- Do the contents provide a clear indication of student's strengths as a prospective classroom teacher?
- Do the contents indicate that the student used classes, assignments, observations, and clinical experiences to think critically about the nature and purposes of schools and learning?
- Do the contents provide a clear indication of student's plans for continued professional development?
- Do the artifacts include necessary integrated documentation of experiences?
- Are written materials in the portfolio free from errors in content and mechanics?
- Is the writing clear and well organized?
- Are the contents well organized, neat, and professional, as well as easy to use?
- Does the portfolio clearly and throughly reflect an understanding of the competencies that is highly persuasive relative to the understanding of intended competency?
- Do the contents reflect substantial evidence of critical assessment and selection of pertinent artifacts with reflections revealing an insightful and thoughtful educator?
- Are the materials appealing, lively, and appropriate, with proficiency demonstrated?
- Are the reflective statements highly persuasive regarding the accomplishment of intended competency?
- Is the portfolio free of glaring errors; grammar, usage, and spelling correct; punctuation smooth?
- Do the personal accomplishments reflect a representation of the student not seen in other artifacts? Do they include shared insights, important details, and a revelation of student's thoughts?

Resource F
Rubrics for Evaluating Portfolios

Name   Institution   Date

3 = Exceeds expectations   Competencies marked 0 are unsatisfactory and
2 = Meets expectations   require additional work. If one zero exists, a fail-
1 = In progress   ing grade will be assigned. The assessor is encour-
                               aged to supplement this form with narrative
                               comments.

Competencies

1. The teacher understands the central concepts and methods   3 2 1 0
   of inquiry of the subject matter discipline(s) he or she
   teaches and can create learning experiences that make these
   aspects of subject matter meaningful for students.

2. The teacher understands how students learn and develop,   3 2 1 0
   and can provide learning opportunities that support their
   intellectual, social, and physical development at all grade
   levels including early childhood, elementary, middle, and
   secondary levels.

3. The teacher understands that students vary in their ap-   3 2 1 0
   proaches to learning and creates instructional opportunities that are adaptable to individual differences of learners.

4. The teacher understands curriculum integration processes   3 2 1 0
   and uses a variety of instructional strategies to encourage
   students' development of critical thinking, problem solving,
   performance skills, and effective use of technology.

5. The teacher uses best practices related to motivation and   3 2 1 0
   behavior to create learning environments that encourage
   positive social interaction, self-motivation, and active engagement in learning, thus providing opportunities for success.

6. The teacher develops a knowledge of and uses a variety of ef-   3 2 1 0
   fective communication techniques to foster active inquiry,
   collaboration, and supportive interaction in the classroom.

7. The teacher plans instruction based on curriculum goals,   3 2 1 0
   knowledge of the teaching/learning process, subject matter,
   students' abilities and differences, and the community; and
   adapts instruction based on assessment and reflection.

8. The teacher understands and uses a variety of assessment 3 2 1 0
   strategies to evaluate and modify the teaching/learning process ensuring the continuous intellectual, social, and physical development of the learner.

9. The teacher evaluates the effects of his/her choices and ac- 3 2 1 0
   tions on others (students, parents, and other professionals
   in the learning community), modifies those actions when
   needed, and actively seeks opportunities for continued professional growth.

10. The teacher fosters positive interaction with school col- 3 2 1 0
    leagues, parents/families, and organizations in the commu-
    nity to actively engage them in support of students' learning
    and well-being.

11. The teacher understands of the importance of assisting stu- 3 2 1 0
    dents with career awareness and application of career con-
    cepts to the academic curriculum.

12. The teacher understands the process of continuous lifelong 3 2 1 0
    learning, the concept of making learning enjoyable, and the
    need for a willingness to change when the change leads to
    greater student learning and development.

13. The teacher understands the legal aspects of teaching in- 3 2 1 0
    cluding the rights of students and parents/families, as well
    as the legal rights and responsibilities of the teacher.

14. The teacher understands the Oklahoma core curriculum 3 2 1 0
    and is able to develop instructional strategies/plans based
    on Priority Academic Student Skills (PASS).

15. The teacher understands the state teacher evaluation pro- 3 2 1 0
    cess, "Oklahoma Criteria for Effective Teaching Perfor-
    mance," and how to incorporate these criteria in designing
    instructional strategies.

Pass _____ Fail _____ Reevaluate _____

Comments:

Portfolio Contents Checklist

The following items must be included, or your portfolio will be returned and an incomplete given until all items are included:

A checkmark indicates that the item was included.

____ 1. Portfolio notebook

____ 2. Handbook in a pocket

____ 3. Updated table of contents

____ 4. Divider pages with tab to reflect three main sections

In Section I include the following:

____ 5. Résumé

____ 6. Current transcript

____ 7. Educational philosophy

In Section II include the following:

____ 8. Individual competencies list

____ 9. Two artifacts for each competency (assigned to this point)

____ 10. Each with explanatory captions and personal reflections

(Note: Use dividers and numbered tabs to label each of the competencies.)

In Section III include the following:

____ 11. Letters of recommendation

____ 12. All formal evaluations and forms from professional field experiences

References

Adorno, T. W. (1989). *Kierkegaard: Construction of the aesthetic.* Minneapolis: University of Wisconsin Press.

Boody, R., & Montecinos, C. (1997, September). Hiring a new teacher? Ask for a portfolio. *Principal,* pp. 34-35.

Bunting, C. (1997). Fostering teacher growth from within. *Principal, 77,* 35.

Campbell, D., Cignetti, P., Melenyzer, B., Nettles, D., & Wyman, R. (1997). *How to develop a professional portfolio: A manual for teachers.* Boston: Allyn & Bacon.

Career Development Center. (1998). *Questions to ask in education interviews* [On-line]. Available Internet: http://www.snybuf.edu/cdc/resume/eduques.htm

College of William & Mary, Office of Career Services. (1996). *Interview questions (teaching)* [On-line]. Available Internet: http://www.wm.edu/csrv/career/stualum/intrwdir/questionteach.html

Doolittle, P. (1994, April). *Teacher portfolio assessment.* ERIC Clearinghouse on Assessment and Evaluation, Washington, DC. (ERIC Document Reproduction Service No. ED 385 608)

East Central University. (1998). *Scoring rubric.* Ada, OK: Education Department.

Evans, M. (1997). *Student portfolio for competency seminar.* Unpublished manuscript, East Central University, Ada, OK.

Family Compliance Office. (1974). *Family educational rights and privacy act.* Washington, DC: U.S. Department of Education [On-line]. Available: http://www.ed/gov/offices/OM/esi.html

Frank, W. S. (1998). *200 cover letters for job hunters: Twenty-eight common mistakes* [On-line]. Available Internet: www.careerlab.com.

Gardner, H. (1993). *Creating minds: An anatomy of creativity seen through the lives of Freud, Einstein, Picasso, Stravinsky, Eliot, Graham and Gandhi.* New York: Basic Books.

Geltner, B. (1993, October). *Integrating formative portfolio assessment, reflective practice and cognitive coaching into preservice preparation.* Paper presented at the annual meeting of the University Council for Educational Administration, Houston, TX.

Gilreath, C. (1997, Fall). *Partial requirement for instructional competency I.* Unpublished manuscript, East Central University, Ada, OK.

Goleman, D., Kaufman, P., & Ray, M. (1992). *The creative spirit.* New York: Dutton.

Habermas, J. (1985). Hermeneutics and the social sciences. In K. Vollmer (Ed.), *The hermeneutic reader* (pp. 293-320). New York: Continuum.

Holton, K. (1997, Spring). *Exit portfolio requirement for professional clinical IV.* Unpublished manuscript, East Central University, Ada, OK.

Hutchins, J. (1997, Fall). *Partial portfolio requirement for instructional competency seminar.* Unpublished manuscript, East Central University, Ada, OK.

Interstate New Teacher Assessment and Support Consortium. (1998). *Model standards for beginning teacher licensing and development* [On-line]. Available Internet: http://www.soe.stthomas.edu/websoew/WHATSHAP/INTASC.html

Interview Experts. (1998). *Interviewing questions* [On-line]. Available Internet: http://www.interviewexperts.com/index.htm

Jacobson, L. (March, 1997). Portfolios playing increasing role in teacher hiring [On-line]. *Education Week on the Web.*

Kalamazoo College. (1998). *Starting a self-presentation portfolio* [On-line]. Available Internet: http://www.kzoo.edu/upfolio

McLaughlin, M., & Vogt, M. E. (1996). *Portfolios in teacher education.* Newark, DE: International Reading Association.

Michalski, R. S. (1987). Learning strategies and automated knowledge acquisition: An overview. In B. Leonard (Ed.), *Computational models of learning* (pp. 1-21). New York: Springer-Verlag.

Morris, V. C. (1969). *Existentialism in education: What it means.* New York: Harper & Row.

Moustakas, C. E. (1981). Heuristic research. In P. Reason & J. Rowan (Eds.), *Human inquiry.* New York: John Wiley.

Murray, D. (1968). *A writer teaches writing: A practical method of teaching composition.* New York: Holt, Rinehart & Winston.

National Board for Professional Teaching Standards. (1998). The portfolio. In *Seeking national board certification* [On-line]. Available on the Internet: http://www.nbpts.org/nbpts/seeking/portfolio.html

Oklahoma State Board of Education. (1996). *Oklahoma general competencies for teacher licensure and certification.* Oklahoma City, OK: Author.

Powers, P., & Currier, C. (1998). *Electronic portfolio assessment* [On-line]. Available Internet: http://www.conknet.com/krsd/krms/EPSE.html

Professional Development Consortia Regions 8 and 11, Los Angeles County Office of Education. (1998). *Portfolios: Students, teachers and electronics* [On-line]. Available Internet: http://www.lacoe.edu/pdc/second/portfolio.html

Sanders, T. (1997, Spring). *Exit portfolio requirement for professional clinical teaching IV.* Unpublished manuscript, East Central University, Ada, OK.

UNL Web Server. (1998). *Career services home page. The structured interview.* [On-line]. Available Internet: http://www.unl.edu/careers/ees/struct.html

University of Colorado. (1998). *School district interview questions for teachers* [On-line]. Available Internet: http://www.cudenver.edu/public/career/tchint97.html

University of Northern Iowa, College of Education. (1998). *Chapter six: Assembling and presenting your professional portfolio* [On-line]. Available Internet: http://www.uni.edu/coe/portfolio/portfolio.html

Wiedmer, T. L. (1998). Digital portfolios: Capturing and demonstrating skills and levels of performance. *Phi Delta Kappan, 79,* 586-589.

Index

CORWIN
PRESS

The Corwin Press logo—a raven striding across an open book—represents the happy union of courage and learning. We are a professional-level publisher of books and journals for K–12 educators, and we are committed to creating and providing resources that embody these qualities. Corwin's motto is "Success for All Learners."